GET REAL

Praise for *Get Real*

Get Real is far more than a good read, it's a call to action. Literally. Today, more than ever, we need leaders to break through the excuse-minded fog that is settling on our society. In *Get Real*, Stephen makes a compelling case that velocity trumps precision while critically reminding us that the journey is the thing.

~ Don Bailey, Financial Services Executive,
New York City, NY.

In Stephen McGhee's new book *Get Real,* he shares an authentic, enlightening and fresh view of leadership that is practical and applicable for everyone. *Get Real* delivers a personal and insightful peek into the lifelong process of leadership development and self-improvement. Leadership learning never ends and I recommend this innovative "how to" book for any entrepreneur, leader or individual who wants to achieve extraordinary life-changing results.

~ Katherine Ott, Chief Executive Officer,
SlimGenics Corporation

Get Real is the literary equivalent to the rubber meeting the road on who you are and who you can be. Each chapter delivers the framework and application of how to align your beliefs and intentions with meaningful action. Stephen McGhee makes it easy to understand why we are capable of much more than we think. Get reading and get living a more powerful and fulfilling life.

~ Tim Brown, Author, *Jumping in the Parade* (2014)

Get Real - A Vital Breakthrough on Your Life and Leadership offers you a genuine challenge: stop thinking about leadership and start leading. Stephen McGhee's newest book teaches us how to get in touch with our often-hidden leadership skills, harness them and utilize them to their fullest potential while bringing out the finest in others. I prescribe *Get Real* for my patients who are ready to take control of their lives, their wellness and their success. Read two chapters and call me in the morning.

~ Kevin Lutz, MD, FACP, Concierge Medical Care,
Denver, Colorado

This is the ultimate how-to handbook for discovering and turning your latent powerful ideas into action. This book is written with such simplicity, honesty and clarity as to be disarming. If you are ready to be disarmed from your defenses to success—this is the place to start. It is a rapid pathway to discovering the self-knowledge that will free you to act on your big ideas and do it now. There is amazing but simple truth here about how to get out of your own way to find success. You will find it a wise and practical manual for creating a mind shift in your life. Kudos to transformational leadership guru Stephen McGhee… a five star effort.

~ William Keiper, Bestselling author
of *The Power of Urgency & Life Expectancy*

If you are ready to take your game to the next level *Get Real* is a must read. Stephen's credibility as a business leader and coach to some of America's most prominent business leaders uniquely positions him to write this book. Apply the principles in this book and get ready to achieve unparalleled results.

~ Norton Rainey, Executive Director of ACE Scholarship

Take ownership of the wisdom Stephen offers in *Get Real* and discover your own path to optimal performance. Throughout my journey, I have yet to discover another person on this planet that is more authentic in helping others achieve their inner peace, clarity and strength. *Get Real* is yet another work of art from a man who cares for us all, and if you possess the will to improve yourself, you too may believe the same.

~ Ken Crowley, former Army Officer
& Professional Athlete

I have been leading teams and organizations for the past 25 years, using traditional leadership models. Since beginning to coach with Stephen McGhee and reading his book, a whole new realm of possibility has opened both personally and in my leadership roles. His leadership ideas and approach are revolutionary. I can already see major improvements in the teams and organizations I lead. I know his coaching and leadership methodology will have a lasting impact on our success moving forward.

~ Tom Fiore

Stephen McGhee is "Hercules of the Heart." Stephen's coaching has empowered me to love deeply, share my gifts courageously and to walk my true path steadfastly. *Get Real* is the heartbeat of truly powerful leadership.

~ Bodhi Kenyon

Knute Rockne once said "One man practicing sportsmanship is better than a hundred teaching it," and the same could be said of Leadership. Stephen speaks with the authenticity of one who has gone to the depths of what leadership means and re-emerges with a practical perspective that is easy to put into action. In fact, it would be hard not to.

~ Anne McGhee Stinson

Your words provided me with constant and driving yet nuanced reasons that one must just get going ... to take the next small step toward living a life of purpose and intention. Each chapter builds on another. Just when I thought you've covered it all, the next chapter peels the onion skin yet again, providing practical and affirming wisdom. Your words are chicken soup for the spirit.

~ Bob Neuman, Chief Dot Connector, BizAdventure

Get Real was a Godsend and landed in my lap at just the right time. I needed this book to remind me that authentic action is always where the rubber meets the road. Obviously, authentic is the key word here and McGhee is refreshingly all that and then some.

~ Dave Zobl, Singer/Songwriter

GET REAL

A Vital Breakthrough on Your Life and Leadership

Stephen McGhee

Get Real
A Vital Breakthrough on Your Life and Leadership
By Stephen McGhee

© Copyright 2014 Stephen McGhee

Published by
Stephen McGhee Leadership, Inc.
1401 Wewatta Street, #315
Denver, CO 80202

Books may be purchased in quantity and/or for special sales by contacting the publisher or author through the website www.mcgheeleadership.com, by contacting: stephen@mcgheeleadership.com or by contacting your local bookstore.

ISBN: 978-1-4936-3780-5

Editors: Steve Chandler, Betsy Osgood
Cover and Interior Design: Nick Zelinger, NZ Graphics
Cover Photo: Marea Evans

FIRST EDITION

Printed in the United States of America

To JR

"Happy is the man who finds wisdom,
and the man who gains understanding."
Proverbs 13, 14

CONTENTS

FOREWORD

Take this plunge
into powerful leadership

The radical health author Paul Bragg wrote quite often about being a member of various "polar bear clubs," whose members would plunge into the ocean in winter to jolt their systems into new levels of clarity and vigor.

Readers of this book by Stephen McGhee will become members of a similar club, a club of people who have taken a most refreshing plunge into the waters of leadership reality.

These waters lie beyond the ego. As McGhee writes, "The ego is focused on creating your image and then protecting that image."

Sounds like a closed system, doesn't it? It is. And this book breaks the ice around that system. This book demonstrates the leadership benefits of getting real.

"Profound change doesn't come from your image," writes McGhee, "it flows from an open heart."

McGhee guides leaders and other powerful and influential people. Most of them—no matter how successful they appear— have never fully understood what is in this book.

Reality is on your side.

It is not against you.

But you have to embrace it, get real, join it, jump in and change how you are leading.

Including how you are leading yourself. It starts right there.

This book is about creating commitments that have more power than your fears. It's about dreaming big and not caring what others think. It's about facing your fears and dwarfing them with big steps of action.

This book throws cold water on the limitations of pragmatism.

Rejuvenating the body with cold water, indoors or out, is an ancient practice for health, stamina and longevity. Kundalini yoga practitioners do this early in the morning, and their name for it is ishnaan.

The ancient Greeks and Spartans practiced it.

This book uses it to rejuvenate the mind.

For example, it throws cold water on your long-held notion that failure is a bad thing, and always to be avoided.

"Don't deny failure," writes McGhee. "Embrace it as if it were your greatest teacher."

Most managers spin their way out of responsibility. They then either sugarcoat or outright hide and lie about the truth they see in the organization.

McGhee is fierce in his rejection of anything but pure authenticity as a leadership practice. He calls it the secret impact of truth telling. This book is an example of walking his talk!

The book is also generously spiced with personal stories and client case histories. Most compelling is his own near-death experience in the hospital when it was discovered that he had a blood clot several inches long. When the doctors lost him and then brought him back, his entire perception of life shifted forever.

After a full recovery, there was new clarity.

"My intention from then on was to live my life in a way that made a difference, not the kind of difference I thought others would approve of."

And he has been true to his word. I know Stephen as a friend, a colleague and as a coach and I also know a number of his clients. They all attest to the bracing nature of his work. How wonderfully refreshing his water is. This book gives you a chance to feel that.

Cold water brings numerous health benefits, including increased peripheral circulation—the blood flow to your skin and the outer parts of the body. It promotes the flushing of toxins.

When you do it to the mind, the same thin happens.

A fully refreshed concept of leadership is now available. This book doesn't just write about that as a concept, it gives you access to it directly. Each chapter finishes with a cold plunge into invigorating action. McGhee invites us to "Get Real!"

Enjoy this experience and share it.

Steve Chandler
Phoenix, Arizona
Winter 2013

1

Enough Visualizing...
Get Moving!

First, I'd like to turn an old idea on its head. I want to suggest that achieving results is the secret to feeling great about yourself. Not the other way around.

I've read and listened to a lot of advice about the laws of attraction, visualization, and positive thinking. They come by many names, but the idea boils down to this: What we believe inspires what we achieve.

Such an approach to leadership has its place, but I'm not here to add to that conversation. Because it misses a central point.

Amid all this talking, thinking and mental processing, it's easy to forget an ingredient without which no one ever accomplishes anything: action.

Of course people who think positively tend to attract more positive results. Absolutely. But if we park too long in this feel-good place, we can lose track of two realities: 1) When positive thinking does lead to success, it never does so without real, specific, decisive *action*, and 2) All successful people experience "failure" as part of their process, and if we blame ourselves for not being positive enough or if we feel pressured to pretend things are great when they're not, then the positive thinking merry-go-round becomes counter-productive.

So, while I sometimes talk about "mindset" in this book, it's only to prepare you for what I really want to deliver. I'm here to give you an informed, experienced boot to the rear, from someone who doesn't just think like a leader, but who knows the kind of action it takes to achieve results.

I'm not here to cheerlead you into merely feeling great about yourself. I want you to actually *do* great things.

So, read on if you're ready to get a move on. Read on if you are ready to create concrete goals, make real plans, take tangible steps toward your objective, stay on task, and achieve measurable results.

A Lesson That Changed My Life

When the teacher called my name, I just sat there, stunned. I couldn't believe it: I was the winner of a national writing contest! It was all the more unexpected because I didn't even know my work had been entered in the contest.

Back then, I found writing easy and natural. When I'd written my essay, I was completely detached from thoughts of competition or winning, because I didn't remember the teacher even mentioning a contest. I just did what I was asked to do, which was to write about the future of the world. To me the assignment was purely fun and creative. I was in the third grade.

Winning that contest felt like an amazing accomplishment for me—until it was taken away.

That moment came when the school principal called me into his office. I had no idea why he wanted to see me. When he asked if I had cheated on the contest, I was dumbfounded. I'd written the story on my own, without outside help or copying. But he kept questioning me, making it clear that he didn't believe me. I asked him why he thought I was a "liar." He replied that the words I used in my story were beyond a third grade vocabulary level, words like "decade," for example.

Instead of congratulating a student who had excelled beyond expectations, the principal seemed more inclined to prove that such excellence wasn't possible.

I was too young to know how to defend myself. I was guilty until proven innocent, and he acted so certain that I gave up.

What could an eight-year-old boy do in the face of adult authority?

As I walked out of his office carrying my Big Chief notepad, I felt sick inside. I felt tainted. From that moment on, I equated writing with pain. I didn't think it was worth the effort to do well at something, if it would only lead to unfair accusations. I did as little writing as possible for more than 30 years.

Has there been a "writing contest" story in your life, a moment along the way when you got the message to shut down an expression of yourself?

It's hard to blame that eight-year-old boy for shutting down. It also seems pointless to blame the principal, just another human prone to mistakes.

But what about the grown man, who, based on a mistake someone else made when he was eight, decided to give up on his gift and hide it from the world?

As a leader, I find it wastes time to place blame or play victim.

I'd rather ask these questions: 1) How can I share my gifts? And, 2) What steps can I take to let go of the past and begin expressing myself again?

Like you, I have something unique to offer…something that only I can offer. We all have something unique to offer. But are we courageous enough to let go of the villains and victims of our past and see ourselves as we truly are, and see our gifts for what they can be?

Children are always learning, and when we grow up, we don't have to stop. The lesson here is one of awareness. My choice of what to do with that moment in the principal's office was available then, and it still remains. I can use that moment as an excuse to shrink from obstacles: injustice, fear of authority, and a belief that effort is rarely rewarded. Or, I can use it as an opportunity to grow into my strengths: a sense of justice, an instinct to stand up for myself, and a gift so exceptional that someone had trouble believing it.

It's not all that important for us to understand why we choose to shut down along the way. Only that we have.

In my leadership work, I often say, "Understanding is the booby prize." It no longer matters what choice you made then. What matters is the choice you make now.

Now is all any of us has. Leadership is presence in action. Good leaders don't waste time blaming themselves or others for their lot in life. They assess what they have to offer now, and create from there.

If you can see your way to that, your next question will be, "What can I create?"

How about whatever is in front of you?

If you were being exactly the person you always wanted to be, what would be the next powerful thing to do?

Why not do that?

I've long since reframed my picture of that moment in the principal's office, so that now I see it as a gift. Every day, that long-ago principal tests my resolve to write and the little boy I once was gives meaning to my words. When I write, I think of him.

The people and moments that challenge us can be our best teachers, if we let them be. These experiences can give us the tools to shape our purpose and to help others shape theirs.

Purposeful Leadership

While creating a positive internal context for our experiences is important, remember, that's just a starting point. It's tempting to become lazy in the name of mental preparation.

Of course introspection and "knowing thyself" can be of significant value in life and leadership. Yet many of us slide into using such "processes" as self-examination, positive thinking, visualization, or even meditation as excuses to rationalize inaction.

Sometimes I catch myself doing it, too.

It's easier to sit on my duff and ponder transforming my life than to actually jump into action and do it.

Our thoughts, feelings, and ideas may spring from our inner selves, but our external actions define us. We can't become much of anything until we do something.

Mental processing is overrated.

As a leadership guide I'm blessed with the opportunity to help people and businesses create results. I love it, because every day I see what works and what doesn't. One thing I've noticed: The difference between no results and results lies in traversing the gap between mental process and purpose—by taking action.

Consider this: every moment starts as a vacuum of space and time. Inside that vortex lies a multitude of choices. Take your pick.

In the end you always have just two choices: the choice between thinking about doing something and actually doing it.

I sometimes sit at my computer and process what I want to write, which isn't a bad thing to do. Thinking before one acts is part of maturity, and planning ahead helps me to better target my actions toward my goal. But waiting for everything to gel perfectly in my mind can leave me staring at a blank screen for so long that the blankness sucks me in.

If my goal is to write an email, blog post, or book, then when it comes to a choice between processing my ideas and writing them down—I have to pick choice number two.

The computer could not care less that I'm facing fear, perfecting an idea, or worrying how my audience will react.

I might write garbage, but I can always edit.

If I just sit there, failure is assured. I don't initiate my purpose until I begin typing.

* * *

Purpose is powerful. It serves you as a leader. But it is badly misunderstood. Most people believe they have to look inward to discover their sense of purpose. And that can take a long time.

Some leaders say to me, "I'm not sure what my purpose is," as if it were some pre-existing quality they had yet to uncover.

Here's what they are missing: We gain a sense of purpose by living on purpose.

If you want to know what your purpose is, here's how you find out: pick one!

Are you worried that you'll pick wrong?

If you're the one deciding, that's not likely. Believe it or not, you do know what's right for you, if you'll just trust your instincts.

So, what would your experience be today if you were fully focused on your purpose?

Most people I work with during those times when they're moving forward on their goals tell me they feel enlivened. They find more depth and meaning in their lives as a whole.

Meanwhile, those without purpose move through days that just grind into one another, with no sense of direction. They are more prone to burnout. They start blaming others for their own lack of enthusiasm.

They simply have no answer to the vital question: Why am I here?

A sense of purpose isn't something you have to wait for. It's something you can choose right now, and once you choose it, it's easy to create the goals that go with it. And once you start moving toward those goals, purpose becomes a self-fulfilling prophecy. You have a purpose because you've chosen one and because you're acting on it.

Some of us question what it means to be "on purpose." Don't worry about figuring it all out. Can you see how the very question pulls you into process rather than execution? That's your ego's way of keeping you on the couch as opposed to serving the world.

Don't just sit there wondering what it all means. Pick a purpose and move toward it. Understanding needn't precede every action. Usually it follows action.

Please don't stand there staring at the abyss all day. You'll psych yourself out. Don't worry that you'll make a mistake if you don't process everything first. You've been developing your values and your character for a lifetime; they're not going to vanish on you now.

*   *   *

Leadership is tricky, because the moment you move with purpose, someone will likely question your process. "Are you sure you've thought this through?" Or worse, "Have you thought of what you'll do if you fail?"

Can you see the hidden trap here? They want to take you off the path of action and back into the world of excessive thinking and self-doubt.

This is your chance to strengthen your commitment to your purpose. Your commitment is to the purpose itself, not the ability to justify it.

Your created sense of purpose is what will give you the resolve to make it through all those moments that call your purpose into question.

If you feel some resistance to this right now, because you find value in processing—don't worry. Your instincts will tell you when you truly do need a moment of stillness.

Meanwhile, while you're in action mode, trust this: Processing never ends, even as you move forward. It's similar to a "loop" in a computer program. Your mind will keep seeking new problems, new solutions, new discoveries, even when you're acting on the one at hand.

Of course, it doesn't hurt to surround yourself with trusted supporters who will call you on it when you're missing the important stuff. Just make sure they're actual supporters, not people who say, "I'm only trying to help" every time they tell you why you've picked the wrong goals.

If you surround yourself with purposeful individuals, there's not much danger there. You know your intentions, you believe in your purpose—you will know who your supporters are.

So, if you want to become the person you can be, here are two questions to ask yourself each morning: 1) What is my purpose today? And 2) What will I do next to convert my purpose into action?

Then go for it.

And when you do, don't hold back.

2

The Swinging Leader

*"Every strike brings me closer
to the next home run."*
~ Babe Ruth

I was sitting at a baseball game last week when something became obvious: Holding back and playing it safe is for sissies! This is even truer when the game is tight.

The same holds true for business leaders in a tough economy. The more leaders play it safe, the more dysfunctional their business performance will be.

When the game is on the line, we all want to see a Babe Ruth step to the plate. Someone who will really swing. Not someone who takes a called third strike while trying to hold for a walk.

Here's something important to consider: Babe Ruth struck out many more times than he hit the ball. Yet what made him a legend? He always came out swinging! He took mighty swing after mighty swing until he slammed a miracle all the way home.

If *you* come out swinging when the odds are against you and when the pitches are tricky, you'll sometimes swing and miss. You'll sometimes strike out. But if you sit at the plate

15

waiting for the easy pitch you miss everything. Even if the pitches are perfect, when you're not swinging you'll strike out anyway.

To continue with the baseball analogy, some people prefer to play it safe and never "go for the fences." Many people rationalize this by calling up the times in the past that they took a chance and lost.

But here's something amazing that neuroscientists have discovered through research: not only do we learn from our mistakes; if we want to become good at something we actually *need* to make mistakes. New neural pathways can't open without them.

We all recognize innovation as a vital element of business success. But the only way to create something new is to risk making a mistake.

So, when you're confronted with a tough pitcher, the best way to figure out how to hit a home run is to swing and miss, perhaps many times.

My life has been filled with free-swinging experiences, based on my adopting the inner spirit that tells me to go for the bleachers. I've struck out many times, but I've always gone on to big wins.

It's not easy to overcome the instinct for safety. The reason for that lies in the same neurological research I mentioned: we learn well from mistakes partly because they upset us. We learn because we never want to do that again.

I'm not suggesting you try every idea that comes along. Not every pitch is worth swinging at. But I am suggesting that there is no winning without courage.

Consider the kind of people who founded this country. America's pioneers were risk-takers—men and women who ventured into unknown territory to shape opportunity from very little capital. They utilized imagination, hard work, and gumption—the kind of gumption that swings for the fences. Their lives were hard. Some failed. But those who flourished turned dreams into reality, making this nation a power to be reckoned with. And the most successful American dreams often had the humblest roots.

Sometimes you can send a ball over the fence without swinging hard, but simply by meeting the ball squarely: taking a chance on something you believe in, when others can't see the possibilities.

Did you know that the recipe for Coca Cola was purchased in perpetuity by an entrepreneur who envisioned customers taking this simple fizzy fountain drink home in a bottle? Nobody else saw that possibility, so he got the deal for one dollar. His family still receives revenue from every can of Coke sold worldwide. Not bad for a one-dollar investment.

The point is that in his day and time that was a ludicrous idea.

What wild, crazy, unhittable pitch will you swing at today?

My sister Anne recently debuted a play called *The Wisdom Within These Walls*. Plenty of people told her nobody would be interested in what a bunch of old people had to say about life's lessons. She ignored the naysayers, and swung away. Her play was an instant home run. After the first weekend, producers were already contacting her about turning it into a movie.

If my sis had played it safe and waited for a better idea to come across the plate, this big success never would have happened. Now, not only has she created an incredible work of art, but also audiences of all ages are receiving inspiration from the wisdom of America's elders.

Get Real

Here's how you can take action today: If you know what you want to do, and you've spent any time processing it, take off the thinking cap and step up to the plate. Just for today, take a chance. Do something that in the past would have scared you into a fever.

If you feel daring, go for that one thing you used to believe you might be great at. Remember that idea of yours? It was the one you were in love with until you let someone else shoot it down.

Learn from your history. Just go for it! Don't let fear run the show. If the thought of going for your goal feels exhilarating, I'm willing to bet you're *on purpose.*

Whatever you decide to do, swing for the fences. You might strike out, or you might surprise yourself. Either way, swinging at the ball is your first step to progress. It's the only way to win.

3

Big Commitment for Big Rewards

The Kid Shares His Secret

The words in the email rang with certainty, like a bell calling a village to wake: "I have discovered the secret to life."

The email didn't say what the secret was.

I grinned. The sender of the email was a young man about half my age. I felt compelled to meet with him to hear what his secret was. I'm glad I did.

I soon learned to love and respect this young man, who possessed a greater wisdom than many people will ever experience.

He had been an alcoholic for much of his brief life, stuffing his pain with anything that would numb his body and mind. His life had plummeted into a downward spiral. His girlfriend had left him, he was estranged from his family, and he'd been fired from a job he loved. He spent most of his time alone. But the booze that once worked to dull the pain was now giving him a life with nothing but pain.

Finally, he got tired of being drunk and lonely. Sick and tired of being sick and tired. So he took an action that would change his life forever. (Action is the sole determinant to performance.)

I think the book and the movie *The Secret* inadvertently misled some people on this subject of change. It led some to believe they could manifest change by simply sitting on the couch and envisioning what they wanted. It rarely works that way. Focusing, visualization, and positive thoughts are a useful beginning, but they can't produce real change. Change doesn't occur until you *do* something.

In this young man's case, his first action was to pick up a book. The book was called *Reinventing Yourself*, written by my close friend and colleague Steve Chandler. Steve himself had suffered from alcoholism, and his book pulled no punches about creating the courage to change.

Inspired by what he read, my young friend stopped whining about the way things were, and started living. Some things continued to be difficult, so he changed what he could, walked away from what he had to, and accepted the rest. He became my friend. Then I became his mentor.

Our path together was not always an easy one. At times he wanted to quit, because it asked him to lean into his growth. It asked him to commit to something better than just getting his life back to normal.

This kind of evolutionary path is rarely comfortable. It can take us to places we didn't expect. Sometimes we emerge from this work as leaders. Soon people are expecting great things from us.

I've seen many people quit when faced with the uncomfortable realization that change creates its own momentum. It's your ego that tells you to quit. Your ego will either tell you that you're perfect as you are, or that you'll never be enough—so, therefore, either way, why bother?

The ego is focused on creating your image and then protecting that image.

But profound change doesn't come from your image; it flows from an open heart. Once your heart has been courageously opened, you realize the exciting possibilities that you have within you.

We all have moments when we want to quit. I've quit many times in my life, on all levels: physically, mentally, emotionally and spiritually. And I've learned something about quitting: it doesn't serve anyone, least of all me.

So why do I quit?

It's simple: change is often slow and difficult, and quitting is quick and easy.

For my young friend, booze was an easy way to "change" his life at first. Like other gratefully recovering alcoholics have said:

"Alcohol gave me wings to fly, but then it took away the sky."

Our society keeps trying to sell us the quick and easy fix. Is it any wonder that so many Americans suffer from depression, addiction and obesity? We want change without action! And when we don't get it, we get frustrated.

I just saw a commercial about a cooking machine that can "turbo cook" your food in seconds. Maybe that works, but I wonder what a machine like that does to food on a molecular level. Many of us want to turbo cook our lives and businesses. But healthy change requires more devoted attention over time.

Transformation requires patience and persistence. It requires finding out what you actually need to do and then doing it. Do you think my young friend simply visualized himself sober and then became that way with no work in between? Of course not. He had to take a hard look at himself, he had to reach out to others, he had to do spiritual work, he had to fight cravings, create goals, get a job, communicate with his girlfriend and his family. In short: he had to take action.

So what was the revelation that coaxed my friend out of the bottom of a bottle and into motion? When I met with him to ask that very question, his hat was pulled down low and tight. But that didn't hide the fact that his eyes were lit up, showing the change ready to burst from him.

"So, what's the secret of life?" I asked.

"The secret to life is facing your fears head on," he said.

It was that simple. But yes, he did explain what that meant for him. The drugs and alcohol "had to do with avoiding my fears," he said. "But I've learned that by facing my fears and not quitting on myself I can have whatever I want in my life."

I agreed, though it was clear he didn't need anyone's agreement. He knew it was true, and he trusted his instincts. Today he has his girlfriend back, he's working at his dream job, he's in great physical shape, and he spends a lot of time with his family. He was right, as he knew he was: When we face our fears, things really do change.

In what ways, have you been avoiding your fears? Have you tried to figure out an easier way to success? Have you been avoiding what you fear? If you want to move from the status quo to success, sorry to break the news: *You'll have to change* in some way.

And if you want to change, you'll have to face your fears. And to really face your fears, you'll have to take action.

Consider the alternative, and where it will lead. Nowhere. So the only question left to ask yourself is, "Am I ready to act?"

Big Huge Dreams

What is your if-I-could-do-anything dream?

Did you already decide that it's so gigantic it's impossible?

Have you come up with an even more sensible reason not to try it, like "the economy is too sluggish"?

"Dream huge" is not just a pump phrase. It's actually a practical and creative exercise. Imagining grand new possibilities is critical to powerful leadership and to human advancement. Many people don't even acknowledge their dreams, for fear they won't come true. Don't believe me? Try asking the next 10 people you meet, "What's your dream in life?" If your experience is like mine, most responders will give you a glazed look, because they don't think about those things anymore. They would have to search some part of their brain they haven't accessed for a while.

We all know that Dr. Martin Luther King had a dream. At the time, his dream of equal rights for people of different races faced seemingly insurmountable odds: an entrenched system of discriminatory laws, economic and educational barriers, ingrained prejudices and fears. Many people thought he was just dreaming. When the civil rights movement he spearheaded made it possible for blacks and whites to drink from the same water fountain, to ride together on the bus, or to go to the same schools—I dare say he succeeded. Dr. King succeeded beyond most people's wildest expectations.

He dreamed big, and that dream was a practical catalyst for change. He was wise enough to know that to make a dream come true requires action. King led a bus boycott, supported a campaign of civil disobedience, went to jail for his beliefs, and marched on Washington. He spoke to hundreds, thousands and ultimately millions. This was a man who dreamed big, then backed it up with practical shoe leather and a decisive voice.

I wonder what it was like for Dr. King to get out of bed each morning with the idea of accomplishing his dream. I'll bet he didn't let his fears stop him from doing what the dream required. I'll bet he jumped out of bed with a sense of purpose.

Living as a leader receives a huge boost when you create an extraordinary dream. Dreams propel leaders into fresh ways of communicating with their people. A dream keeps a leader edgy, authentic and inspired.

I remember a meeting in which I asked a client to express his huge dream. He'd given the idea considerable thought, and it didn't take him long to list several gigantic dreams. Were they all realistic? Maybe not. That's the point. His dreams were so big that I know, and he knows, he'll never accomplish some of them. But all he needed was for one of them to capture his imagination and set him into motion.

So, I dropped the billion-dollar question: "Who would you have to be as a leader to make that dream happen?"

You could have heard a pin drop, as I watched him picture that person.

Then I challenged him, "Why not just start being that person today?" His face took on a glow and his shoulders stretched back, as he imagined himself *being* the man he'd always wanted to be. From that moment on, he began to practice living his life from that place.

To be a good leader you must act. But to act effectively, you must first know what you want, believe you can get it, and become the kind of person who can make it all happen.

Therefore great leaders become good at *being*. If you want to lead people toward a dream, you must first become that dream to show them the way.

You can start being that person right now. How? Don't worry, once you give yourself permission to believe you can manifest a dream, then that belief will give you the power to behave in the way the dream requires.

The brain is funny that way. Neuroscientists can tell you that the brain responds to imagined stimuli and real stimuli as if they were both the same. Both responses cause a physiological reaction.

Want to give that theory a little test? Take a bite of an imaginary lemon right now. Really picture a very real lemon being bitten into by you. What happens? Do your lips pucker? Does your mouth water? Can you see and feel the lemon?

You can see and feel your dream.

If you want to be the kind of leader who can achieve a dream, then decide you are…and you will be.

Dreams do come true. Leaders make them come true all the time. My clients can testify to that. If you envision your dream, if you're willing to become the person who can make it happen, and if you take action as if it were a real possibility—you can make it real. But only if you commit.

The Truth On Commitment

Everything we do starts with a thought. So if you want to perform as the best at what you do, start thinking of yourself as someone capable of being the best. Then ask yourself: "What are the actions of someone who is the best?" Then take those actions. Then keep taking those actions. Never give up on taking those actions, no matter how tough it gets. That's what a personal internal commitment is all about: a promise to follow through. Commitment transforms your promise into reality.

The very word "commitment" is a turnoff for many people. We often put the brakes on somewhere between the dream and the commitment. Many societal cues have taught us that commitment is a kind of death: giving up our freedom, painting ourselves into a corner, giving in to other people's demands.

It's tempting to buy into the false idea that commitment will require us to give up our independent sense of self.

But consider this alternative view: Committing to something may actually be the fastest way to achieve freedom.

As a life-and-business consultant, I often ask people what they want in life. As often as not, they answer, "Money." When I ask what money will do for them, they reply, "Money will buy me freedom."

Okay, but notice this: To get that money, you need to take action. Therefore freedom is the ability to act in pursuit of your dreams. And how can we do that effectively if we don't commit?

Committing doesn't mean being forced to do what other people demand of you. It's the opposite of that. You own your commitment. It's your creation. It allows you to fully pledge yourself to a dream.

Freedom isn't easy. It's often hard. It can be hard to commit to change, to commit to a dream, to commit to action. But consider the alternative. Because, where there's action, there's life. We are most alive when we are in joyful action.

But when we are stuck and decomposing from inaction, there's a slow death: spiritual, emotional, mental, and eventually physical death.

Our parents and teachers, in the name of good manners and getting along, have taught us that we're not the center of the universe, that we need to make room for others, to share, to be humble.

Unfortunately we sometimes take those lessons to extremes—assuming that to be humble we have to hold back and never put ourselves first. We have to avoid assert-ing ourselves around others. So when we give a less than stellar performance, it's easy to rationalize that it was all in the name of humility, teamwork, or following the rules. Keeping a low profile and not making waves become our core social beliefs.

Beliefs are powerful. When we believe something, it becomes the foundation of our decision-making processes, and our actions. So, if you're going to live your life accord-ing to a belief system, why not build that system with beliefs that radically support achieving your goals?

Try this one on for size: "I am courageous."

No one can stop you from believing that belief.

Of course it is also possible to make a personal internal commitment to simply "survive." Back when humans had to escape sabertooth tigers and spear woolly mammoths, survival itself was quite an accomplishment.

But is survival all you want today? In this magnificent global market full of infinite opportunity? If it is, then commit to "just getting by," and you know what? You'll succeed. You'll train your mind, heart, and body to produce the vision, the ideas, and the actions that lead to mediocre but acceptable performance.

If, however, you make a personal internal commitment to be outstanding at something, then everything in your life—seen and unseen—will move you forward to fulfill that commitment.

In May of 1940, Winston Churchill addressed the British House of Commons as the armies of Adolph Hitler were roaring across Europe on their way to obliterating England.

If you want to get a good feel for what a dream backed by a commitment looks like, look to these words boomed out by Churchill on that day:

"I would say to the House, as I said to those who have joined the government: 'I have nothing to offer but blood, toil, tears and sweat.'

"We have before us an ordeal of the most grievous kind. We have before us many, many long months of struggle and of suffering. You ask, what is our policy? I will say: It is to wage war, by sea, land and air, with all our might and with all the strength that God can give us; to wage war against a monstrous tyranny, never surpassed in the dark and lamentable catalogue of human crime. That is our policy.

"You ask, what is our aim? I can answer in one word: victory; victory at all costs, victory in spite of all terror, victory, however long and hard the road may be; for without victory, there is no survival. Let that be realized; no survival for the British Empire, no survival for all that the British Empire has stood for, no survival for the urge and impulse of the ages, that mankind will move forward towards its goal.

"But I take up my task with buoyancy and hope. I feel sure that our cause will not be suffered to fail among men. At this time I feel entitled to claim the aid of all, and I say, 'Come then, let us go forward together with our united strength.'"

Committing to your dream also entitles you to claim the aid of all those who can help you. Ask for what you want. Pray for what you need. Let people be inspired by what you are up to in life. Look at how many people jumped at the chance to help Dr. King. Look at the help Churchill got from Franklin Roosevelt and the United States and so many others.

That decisive help came from the willingness to declare a commitment to a dream.

This commitment of yours doesn't just benefit you. It will enliven and benefit everyone you come in contact with. Your inspired *way of being* inspires those around you to make the best of themselves.

The urge to become more than we've been is interwoven into our very souls. It is evolution itself. The blooming and blossoming of all living things. So dig deep and come up with a dream that asks you to get close to greatness. Your soul is just waiting for a chance to rise to that occasion.

Get Real

Here's how you can take action today: Write down one fear that has stopped you from pursuing your dreams in the past. Now write down the answer to this question: what huge dream would I pursue without my fear? Now make a personal internal commitment to that dream. To make it feel real, write your commitment down, too. Use the words "I commit," or "I pledge" or "I promise." After you've written all this down, take one more step: write down one action you'll take this week that will force you to face your fear, and that will take you one step closer to your dream. Then go do it!

— Blog to Blunt Moms about
 DD oregon

write a blog post for DRS
about my first Grand trip

4

Become Extraordinary...
One Ordinary Step at a Time

The Ordinary Path to Becoming Extraordinary

What does it take to become extraordinary? The answer to this life-long question posed by the ambitious, the dreamers, the seekers, is wonderful in its simplicity: You become extraordinary *by being ordinary*.

Contradiction? Not really.

After I landed my first professional job, I remember wearing new shoes to the orientation. They hurt like hell, but man, they were shiny! To me, they seemed to say, "Here's a guy on the path to success."

When the president of the bank came in to talk with us, I noticed that his shoes were shinier than mine. In fact, everything about him seemed to shine and say, *Here's a guy who has already reached success.*

He inspired me. I wanted to impact people like that, to shine, to be extraordinary. I wondered, looking at my role model for success, what huge quantum leaps he had taken to get where he was.

The most significant question inside me that day, a question many people have asked me since, was this: How do I, myself, become extraordinary like that?

After 25 years of experience and mistakes, I can now tell you the answer: There are no magic quantum leaps...the key to becoming extraordinary is to be *willing to do the ordinary.*

If you think focusing on one ordinary action after another sounds boring, I'll confess I used to agree. But I now realize that the practice of achieving extraordinary results through ordinary steps represents incredible freedom. It's such a relief to focus on the next step and not carry the entire future in your head every moment.

Whether I was pursuing a business project, a friendship, or climbing Aconcagua—my most amazing experiences have come from the simple discipline of putting one foot in front of the other. That has been the simple key to summiting extraordinary peaks, personal and professional.

How would you respond right now if someone asked, "Are you extraordinary?" Maybe you'd want to seem confident so you'd quickly say, "Sure! I have something special to offer."

What you need to know is that even if you don't fully believe your answer: you're right. You do have something very special to offer. And you also know what it takes to be an effective leader.

The process is simple: it takes 1) Figuring out what we want, 2) Making a plan to get there, and then 3) Applying ourselves to take on one ordinary task at a time, each and every day.

For extraordinary people, most days are filled with seemingly ordinary tasks. But they enjoy brief, shining moments of victory along the way—and those moments imbue the other moments with a sense of purpose that gives joy and meaning to life.

Take an Olympic swimmer who wins a gold medal. When you see that moment of glory, don't forget: it's the result of hundreds of mornings of waking early, swimming on hot days and cold days, and repeating the same ordinary motions over and over until exhausted. It involves traveling to swim meets, and listening to repeated instructions from coaches. It is a result of years of training day-in and day-out. It represents years of repeating such ordinary thoughts as: "Don't give up! Keep going! You can do it!"

Are you willing to do ordinary things to obtain an exceptional result?

I often work with people who want exciting results, but who seek to avoid boring or tedious effort. To those people, I say, "Get real."

Consider the courage it takes to always take the next ordinary step toward your goal. We cheer for winners because we know how hard it is to keep doing the ordinary without the promise of instant gratification.

You can win, too. All you have to do is fully understand the power of the ordinary.

Excellence

Practice leads to precision, and precision leads to excellence. If you want a reminder of how the consistent practice of leadership creates results, I recommend spending an evening at a concert featuring your local symphony orchestra. As the beautiful music pours over you, let yourself meditate upon the precision required to bring together such a large band playing all those disparate instruments, from wind, to percussion, to strings.

Then let yourself realize that the foundation of such extraordinary precision is ordinary practice! Even though the end results are absolutely magical.

When I'm at the symphony, it's easy for me to imagine that the conductor doesn't need to be there. The musicians are skilled, they know their parts, and they know how to count. Surely they can do it without him!

But as a lifelong student of great leadership, I understand that the conductor's silent presence and his seemingly casual waving of the baton actually represent weeks, months, even years of the persistent application of his knowledge of music, his vision for each piece, and his understanding of teamwork—in short, the application of leadership.

To achieve mastery of any skill requires thousands of hours of practice.

Leadership is no different.

The best conductors aren't only master musicians, but masterful leaders as well.

The same is true of the best corporate executives, small business owners, educators, artists, scientists, politicians, and more. Moments of harmonious precision occur often in their lives because of their long-term willingness to practice.

Sage leaders throughout history have spoken of finding excellence in simple things. The beauty of an orchestra's precision is that every little note is played with a unique application of time and intensity. Those details only come into focus through a commitment to practice: alone, at rehearsals, under the guidance of the conductor, in cooperation with the orchestra. The musicians aren't just practicing notes; they're also practicing their ability to take criticism, to listen to each other, to shut out distractions, and to press on when they don't feel inspired.

Much of our world is wired for seeking comfort and avoiding effort. That's why it is truly extraordinary when someone commits to the constant practice of excellence.

A company might try to guarantee customer satisfaction, but often when I request that such a company make good on that promise, a customer service agent will treat me with annoyance. It's easy to promise excellence; it's not easy to consistently practice the steps to achieve it.

Sitting at the concert it occurs to me that a great symphony has virtually the same qualities I like to find in a great business. The perfection that I hear when I listen to my favorite orchestra isn't just because of individual talent, or technical skill, or chance—it's rather a result of coordinated and inspired *intention*. The leader guides everyone toward the same intention, and they all apply themselves consistently to harmonize and realize that intention.

Sometimes I well up with emotion when I experience such magnificence, because I recognize the hours of practice that went into the performance. I can imagine the many short-term pleasures the participants gave up, and all the "dull and ordinary" steps they had to repeat daily…steps that they made sacred and special.

The Very Next Step

The gun went off. The excitement in the air was palpable. Every runner was fleet of foot as he ran the first few steps of Colorado's Imogene Pass footrace.

This storied, traditional race covers 17 miles of beautiful but grueling terrain from Ouray to Telluride. Runners make a 10-mile ascent to a summit of over 13,000 feet, before plunging into a seven-mile descent down loose rock and winding jeep track. This is not a race for the faint of heart. But then that's why so many runners participate year after year.

Living life to its fullest potential is like running the Imogene Pass race.

Because living a full life is not for the faint of heart, either (and why would we want it to be?). In life, there are steep ascents and descents. There are hard times. For all of us. But is this the bad news?

Not if you want to live to the fullest.

Because hard times always take us to transformative places we would not otherwise go. The hard times make us strong enough to reach the good times. The hard times make the good times feel even better.

The Imogene race can be a great metaphor for any difficult goal. Once we make the commitment to run, the first steps seem easy. As we begin the race, we're excited, and so is everybody else.

Then, shortly into the steep uphill push, reality sets in.

OMG, what was I thinking?

Running Imogene Pass over the years has pushed me through a host of challenging emotions. Sometimes when my lungs and calves were burning, I asked myself, "Why the hell am I taking on this ridiculous pass when I don't have to?"

Even if you don't run, no doubt you can relate. You take on things and they are harder than they looked.

Maybe you start a new relationship, a business venture, or community project, believing it will be easy! Or maybe you worried that it would be difficult, but were surprised at how easy it was—at first. Till reality arrived.

Business projects run a similar trajectory. At the beginning everything seems possible, as we take the first easy steps toward our vision. Then the first obstacle appears, or we grow complacent, or we stop wanting to practice the ordinary steps toward an extraordinary goal we've begun to doubt. We question whether we have what it takes. Should we keep going? Have we set our sights too high? Do we need an easier goal?

One year when I was running up Imogene Pass, the high altitude, the steep terrain and lack of sleep all began to gang up on me. I was so sick with fatigue I thought I would vomit. My body ached and my feet bled from the blisters forming in my wet socks. *Of course* I wanted to quit. I pictured slipping into the forest, knowing the other runners would assume I was just making a pit stop. No one would know I'd quit.

Except me, of course.

Then I glanced at an older gentleman running near me. He was lean and muscular, with a grey beard and shoulder-length hair. His eyes glimmered with purpose and God's light. When he turned those eyes on me, they registered my pain. My eyes were swollen with threatening tears, and he knew it. He placed a gentle but firm hand on my shoulder, and when I turned toward his loving smile he said, "Just take the next step, my friend...then the next one. You'll get there." That was all.

Through my pain, I felt his wisdom sink into my core. My mind shifted so fast, I almost heard it click. I took the next step, and the next, and suddenly I was picking up the pace. Though he didn't speak again, I could feel him running near me. I felt two spirits uniting in the purpose of stepping forward. I began feeling strong, so strong that my angel friend and I caught up with the pace group I thought I'd lost for good!

When we reached the summit, I searched for my bearded friend.

He was nowhere to be found.

I never saw him again. He was there when I needed him, then he moved on.

But he lives in me today. I would not have finished that race without the support of my bearded friend. The inspiration he gave me that day, which I have put to work in many ways ever since, was: "Just take the next step, my friend."

My work as a leadership visionary has allowed me to pay that wisdom forward many times. The next time you fear you're not going to make it, imagine my hand on your shoulder and my voice in your ear, saying, "Just keep stepping."

Don't think about the next 17 miles, or 17 days, or 17 hurdles. You'll wear yourself out. Just think about the next step, and take it. Then do it again.

It's not easy. But it *is* simple. As John Roger said, "He or she that endures to the end wins."

The Momentum of Motion

As you keep taking one step after another, you'll notice that things work best when you're feeling momentum.

At times we all need to slow down, or just pause, to catch our breath. But be careful not to stop for long, because the most effective actions take place when we're feeling that flow, that rhythm. That's when we're most likely to achieve the successes that lead us to say, "I'm on a roll!"

We all know the feeling that says, "If I sit down, I'll never get up!" All successful journeys are like that, whether the sitting down is literal or figurative. There always comes a moment when we want to pack it in, because the work it will take to get there is beyond what we imagined.

When that happens, don't think about all the work ahead. Just ask yourself, "Can I take one more step?"

Sure you can.

Need a breath? Fine. Take two. Just don't sit down. Don't stop for long. Because once you stop it's too easy to stay stopped.

Sir Isaac Newton's first law of motion basically states that a body at rest tends to remain at rest, and a body in motion tends to remain in motion, unless acted on by an external force.

This is also true of human activity.

So if you want to reach your objective, keep moving. Otherwise, it could take a lot of work to pry you from that state of rest.

Many Americans are so excessively busy you may question their need for this advice. Aren't they always in motion?

But what kind of motion is it?

I'm not talking about going through motions for their own sake. I'm talking about *forward* momentum.

"It is not enough to be busy," said Henry David Thoreau. "So are the ants. The question is: What are we busy about?"

Some motions people go through in life are merely circular. These motions take them back to the same points every day: bed to kitchen to car to work to kitchen to couch to bed, and back. But leaders, while they might go through some of those motions, also take motions that create upward momentum. They learn a new skill, visit a new country, start a new project, create a new business, and then they keep moving to execute and implement those new things.

Some people step outside the circular dance now and then simply to laugh, love, and play. That's life-giving momentum, too.

Whatever you're busy doing, ask yourself: Am I moving forward in a meaningful way toward my vision? If the answer is yes, then keep moving in that direction, at the pace that suits your goal.

Velocity has a grace and flow that can create a joyful atmosphere. Do you remember the last time you worked on a project that had that kind of momentum? The very air around everyone involved felt electrified, didn't it?

As a leader, that's the environment you want to deliberately and consciously create. You don't just wait for it to happen.

The way you create that momentum is to keep stepping at a steady pace. Not just when it's easy—there's no need to work on that, is there? The easy stuff? The important thing is to keep stepping when it's hard. The only way to stay inside the flow is by always stepping over the obstacles and through the challenges.

At times I've had to reach into my gut for the courage to take the next step. It can hurt physically and emotionally, whether I'm climbing a mountain, attending a meeting, or Speaking to a large group.

That next step is where the maturity of leadership prevails. You will grow as you keep stepping past the limitations you perceive yourself to have. That's why many leaders become physically and mentally stronger as they get older: not because their body or brain is at its peak, but because they step through the pain and fear and know they can do it again.

We can make life easier by only focusing on the next ordinary step. Everything worthwhile in life offers the opportunity to discover grace in each and every step. If you need a reason to take the next step, envision your reward: the extraordinary achievement of true self-satisfaction and service to others.

Get Real

Stop for a moment and consider an area of your life that, on a scale of one to 10, you can envision moving from a seven to a 10. What would the result be? How would you feel? Write down your answer on a slip of paper and stick it in a drawer. OK, now that you can envision the result, back up and ask, "What would be just one ordinary step I would have to practice every day to take me closer to that goal?" Write down your answer to this second question on a second slip of paper, and post it somewhere where you'll see it every day.

Now, I invite you to create something extraordinary, by doing something ordinary: tomorrow, take the simple step you posted, just once. Then the next day, take that same step again. Just focus on repeating that one step you've committed to for this week. Just take the next step, my friend. You'll get there.

Next week, if you haven't yet reached the goal, do this exercise again, and pick a new step.

Repeat.

5

Play Your Own Music

Pause Has Value Too

If you pay close attention, you'll notice that the momentum of any project, any career, any relationship, heck, any life—has its own internal rhythm.

In any rhythm there are up beats and down beats. You need both to keep the rhythm going. Just as it's important to remember to keep stepping, especially when the going gets tough, it's also important to be willing to pause and to listen.

What I am going to suggest doing can sometimes be difficult for people on a roll to do: Stop and be still for a while.

Yes…for at least a few minutes, but preferably for an hour or so. External stillness can be nice, but if you fall asleep while sitting still, then at least seek internal stillness, while you go for a walk or a yoga class or a drive…or whatever leaves your mind open, receptive, and relaxed.

Pause long enough to evaluate who you are, where you are, and where you're trying to go. Pause to consider whether you're still on the best path to get from point A to point B. But, and here's the tricky part, in these quiet moments don't worry so much about specific answers, rather just let the ideas and sensations of self wash through you.

This is the other side of the momentum we talked about earlier. When you're stepping forward, there's a certain momentum or rhythm to that. But when you pause, that too is a vital part of the rhythm. So, make sure that, wherever your life is, it's in keeping with your true rhythm.

How do you know when you're staying true to your rhythm? This requires deep honesty. Putting it in more practical terms: on the one hand, don't be in such a hurry to move forward that you fail to stop and take assessments of your progress along the way; on the other hand, don't pause so long that you become paralyzed by inaction and an inability to choose.

Finding the proper rhythm on the road to success is like breathing out and breathing in. Both are necessary and restorative.

Sometimes when we need to choose the next steps toward a goal, we remain uncertain of which choice is best even after all the information is in. Don't let that tempt you to stare into the abyss too long. That's when you're in danger of letting fear take over the decision-making process. Trust your gut to tell you when it's time to simply make a choice and move on.

If you're honest with yourself, you'll know when you're hesitating too long over a decision. It's when you've stopped weighing options and started letting fear take over.

If there's no way to know which choice is best, just choose, and keep the momentum going.

Remember that you have a lot to say about whether your choice was a "good" one. Many an unwise choice has been converted by a creative leader into a brilliant outcome.

It's more important to make the decision, for better or worse, and keep the rhythm of performance snapping along, than to sit still and wait for every last shred of evidence to support a decision. It's rare we get to make decisions with every last fact in hand.

Sometimes we really do have to take our best shot, and joyfully wing it.

The Rhythm of Leadership

Whether we ourselves remain in constant motion, or stuck on pause, the beat goes on, my friends. It always goes on. So, as a leader you must learn to listen for that rhythm, in motion and at rest.

When you're working toward a goal and everything is falling into place, can you hear the rhythm that accompanies that? Sometimes you can feel the rhythm when you're in the midst of a flurry of activity. You find every move you make is a dance step to that rhythm, part of a larger pattern you can sense. But when all your actions and their results reach a crescendo, sometimes that's the cue that you need to follow up with some silence. Only you can see the complete pattern, only you can feel and hear all the music, its notes and harmonies and rhythms—if you set aside time for stillness and silence.

Most of us are in too big of a hurry to tune in to our own rhythms, much less the rhythms of the projects, relationships, and activities we move in and out of throughout our lives. Although I believe that pursuing my purpose requires me to keep on stepping and maintain momentum, I've also found that when I get into too big a hurry, I can miss some of the best songs in life. Those songs can teach me even more about my purpose. So now and then, I stop and listen.

If I don't listen to what my life is singing to me, I risk missing golden opportunities. Ideas and people and possibilities run toward me and away, or I run toward this one and that, without focus, unable to decipher what's important. It's like being in a big game of tag, where one thing after another becomes "it." I don't know what or who to chase, and just run after anything that presents itself. "Tag, you're it." "No, you're it." "Now you're it!" When I run around like that, without clear direction, then life is no longer full of rhythm or music. It's just a mayhem of ideas, dreams and possibilities to temporarily chase, never following through on any.

I might try to force order on all that mayhem by imposing an external rhythm, but if I fail to stop and quietly listen to the harmonies already within me, I still get nowhere. Perhaps it's no longer a confusing game of tag; now it's just an endless checklist of to-do items, with no sense that it's all leading toward any meaningful purpose.

When I get exceedingly busy, without pausing to ask my soul what it wants or why, even my personal relationships become more items on a to-do list. I'm not trying to be obscure with this metaphor. I'm just trying to say to you that sometimes following the right path requires a sense of self that can't be easily defined or quantified. It requires listening to all those unspoken, invisible cues in your life. It requires a trust in your inner sense.

This is what I mean by listening to the rhythm of your world, and listening to your own internal music.

I remember going to a concert just a few years ago that featured the late '70s/early '80s band Styx. Some of you won't remember them, but you'll still get my point. When I went to that concert, the band had been around for 30 years! It was a night of nostalgia, but soon it hit me that whether they were playing old tunes or new, everything they played sounded unusual and interesting. Even after all these years, the audience was completely taken with them. Styx brought down the house.

I asked myself, "How has this rock band stood the test of so much time?"

The answer was simple: they always were, and they have remained, true to their internal music. They have always maintained that trust in their inner sense. They continued to play and sing their songs in their own inimitable way.

Music that imitates, or that lacks internal integrity, does not have a 30-year following.

It's the same way with leaders in all fields. If you're a copycat, people won't dig your "music." Leaders in music, or in any other walk of life, become great influencers of people when they follow their own authentic rhythm.

As a leadership coach, I often see people's eyes light up over someone else's great idea. I listen to these clients consider at length how they might repeat someone else's success. Often I discover that this eagerness to imitate covers up a fear just under the surface, a fear of starting from scratch, or taking a risk and testing their own ideas in the marketplace. They fear failure so much that they'd rather reinvent someone else's wheel. These are people who try so hard to copy the music of others that they lose track of the original tunes they carry inside.

Then there are those who are attached to other people's belief systems about success, people who see public approval as the measure of their worth. Such people fear pursuing any ideas that might cause other people to reject them or laugh at them. They fear that someone will tell them they're unrealistic dreamers, or lacking in talent, or that such goals are only attainable by people with the right connections or clout. These, too, are people who've forgotten how to listen to their own internal rhythm.

The point is: you're already and always an original. Each and every one of us is. Go with it. Inspire people with how true you are to your inner compass.

Leaders aren't leaders because they stand in front of a group of people and force them to follow. Leaders are leaders because they listen to their internal rhythm and follow it.

Sometimes they find others whose rhythms harmonize with theirs and spend time playing with those others. But while leaders may listen to the rhythms of others, learn from them, and share in them, they don't try to shape those rhythms into their own. They don't try to sing someone else's song. That's never as powerful as creating something original.

Within you lies an original style of leadership, if you have the courage to listen to it, to practice it, and to perfect it. You may not ever make it as big as The Beatles, or Styx, or Dave Matthews. Or you might make it bigger! The only thing you can be sure of is that nobody can sing your song better than you.

The thing is, no one is likely to ask you to sing until after you show them you can sing. The only way to do that is to open your mouth and cut loose.

Don't hold back. Let it rip and sing it loud. You have nothing to lose, except unnecessary pride. You have everything to gain, including the possibility of success beyond your dreams.

Authentic leaders don't hide their talent. Authentic leaders courageously put themselves out there. Authentic leaders are even prepared to fail in society's eyes, if that's what it takes to succeed at being themselves.

It doesn't matter if your song isn't perfect, so long as it isn't fake. Humans have an instinctive ability to spot a phony, sooner or later. So why hold back from your true self?

Not sure who your true self is? Like I said, sometimes you need to stop running around trying to do, do, do, and instead sit still and just listen. Listen to God, and He will tell you who you are. That will tell you your great idea for a song, or will nudge you in the direction of other authentic musicians who will help you find your way.

My life is devoted to singing my song. If people don't want to listen, they don't have to.

I've discovered something interesting, although I suppose it seems obvious in retrospect: when you start singing your song, the kind of people who like your kind of music begin to show up, as if by magic. And other people? No need to worry about them; they go somewhere else to get their music fix.

If you want to succeed, your first step is to listen to your song, and your second is to understand its power. Another way to put that is that you must trust your soul. Your soul recognizes the ideas that are right for you and those that aren't. Your soul knows which leadership skills are your strengths and when to use them.

Listen carefully to your own inner wisdom. If you're willing to slow things down, it will speak to you. It will sing to you. It wants to be heard. Once you find that inner voice, you can begin to practice singing along, to the rhythm of your unique, original, unduplicatable self.

Get Real

Do you keep a calendar or to-do list? If you do, grab it and have it handy. If you don't, create one just for this week. When you have your calendar or to-do list in hand, do this: find a free hour in this week's schedule, and if you don't have one, create one. Now write down the following task for that free hour:

Be silent and still, as you consider your creative strengths, your possible ideas, and/or your leadership skills.

At the end of the hour select a creative idea, endeavor, or service you've been withholding from others, whether because of self-doubt, or lack of self-awareness, or any other reason. Then, find a place on next week's calendar to take a first step toward acting on the idea, endeavor, or service you've been withholding.

As you do this exercise, do you realize that there's some area of work, relationships, or play where you may have been appeasing? If so, and if necessary, schedule a meeting or phone call to create alignment with that person.

During the hour you've spent listening to self, can you see that at times you may have put on a show for others. Don't feel bad; it happens to the best of us. Be grateful you've discovered the truth, and take this new opportunity to change your life.

A week after your session of quiet listening, make note of any changes you experience. If you like those changes, or see potential in them, I suggest you schedule yourself regular down times to stop and listen to the music, the music of your own soul.

———————

6

From "What's Wrong?" to "What's Next?"

A Vision of the Future

Your future can only be bright if you can communicate it in bright ways. If you spend most of your time communicating to yourself and others about the mistakes, failures, and injustices of your past, the future becomes harder to create.

This might sound obvious, yet many of us get stuck.

There are generally two kinds of communication. The first kind focuses on what has gone wrong before. In "what went wrong" communication, the speaker comes from a position of having been victimized by circumstances or people, and focuses on what didn't work.

This kind of communication usually leads to predictions that things will likely go wrong again in the future, based on "what went wrong" in the past.

The second kind of communication focuses on possibility. In the communication of "what is possible," the speaker comes from a position that, whatever happened in the past, the future is wide open. This kind of thinking does not focus on the failures of the past, nor does it *ignore* them. It simply includes both what *has* worked and what *hasn't* worked as information that might be useful in setting up new parameters to reach future goals—with the attitude that they are achievable.

The communication of "what is possible" also includes an element not available in the communication of "what went wrong," and that is: imagining a possibility that we've never considered before, even when there is no evidence for it in our experience.

This is how scientists make breakthrough discoveries, how teachers get through to students other people have written off as hopeless, and how inventors create conveniences we suddenly can't live without.

I'm not here to judge the people who make either type of communication. My only interest is in what works and what doesn't. As a consultant and guide to leaders, I've become a sort of scientist of communication: carefully observing the words, actions, and results of my clients as they walk their leadership paths.

I've listened to hundreds of leaders create their futures. Those acts of creation always start with thoughts which I can't see. But after the initial thoughts, everything else they do is observable: what they say, what they do, and the results they achieve.

Here's what I've observed: Those who succeed are those who most often communicate in terms of "what is possible."

I'm not saying that those who see possibilities in every challenge don't ever fail, or that those who point out impossibilities in the face of every suggestion don't ever succeed. But it has become clear to me that people who spend more time talking in terms of possibility and challenges, instead of impossibility and obstacles, are the most likely to achieve a magnificent future.

When we accept that the more we live in the past, the more we handicap our ability to create powerful results—an internal freedom emerges. This does not mean we start floating toward some great future buoyed on the lighter-than-air magic of positive thoughts alone. The kind of freedom I'm talking about is driven by an inner desire to create the future we want, and it's founded on the knowledge that to create that future we must act on it. We can't just think optimistic thoughts. We must discipline ourselves to walk through every real-life step it will take to turn our dream into a reality.

Let me take that a step further. I encourage you to consider a future so big that you don't yet have *any* idea how to fulfill it.

This is what President John F. Kennedy did in 1961, when he declared that the United States would land a man on the moon within the decade. He had no clear idea at that moment how to achieve that goal; he was not a rocket scientist. But he could imagine it and powerfully communicate the possibility as a commitment.

In 1969, the possibility he imagined came true: Neil Armstrong stepped onto the moon and uttered those famous words, "One small step for a man, one giant leap for mankind." Such is the power of our imagination, when we dedicate ourselves not only to seeing the vision, but also to figuring out the steps to get there, and then actually taking them.

If you want to blow yourself away, declare a future so big it will transform both your life and the lives of others. Dream big enough, and the future you envision will *want you*. It will pull you into its path with miraculous power.

Sometimes people will set obstacles in your way. Sometimes circumstances won't be optimal. Sometimes bad luck will strike. The trick to moving toward a grand vision is not to deny reality, but to stop dwelling on how "right" you are about who or what has "wronged" you. That kind of thinking has no value in problem solving or goal setting.

Yes, of course other people should take responsibility for their actions; accountability is important. But you cannot force others to act in the ways you want them to act. The best you can do is to do the best you can do. Why waste time standing around contemplating the damage others have done along the way? Blaming others might make us feel better for a moment, if all we're trying to do is survive. I don't know about you, but that's not enough for me.

Most leaders I know became successful because they were interested in something beyond mere survival, beyond avoidance of pain. They became successful because their life was to make a difference.

A goal like that can become a self-fulfilling prophecy. When you say you want to make a difference, and when you then choose a goal with the power to make a difference, and when you move on to take the actions that lead to that goal—how can you help but make a difference?

Once you have identified a future worthy of your attention, I encourage you to share it with people. Share it with people whose support will help you create that future. Do *not* share it with naysayers—those people who spend most of their time communicating about "what went wrong" and "what will go wrong." Rather, share your vision with other people who deal in "what is possible."

Please understand, when I tell you to share it, I don't just mean that you should simply chat about it. I'm talking about powerfully declaring your intention. The power of your declaration (like the power of President Kennedy's) will inspire others to support and share that intention.

I'm talking about communicating in a deep way, not just about what you want to achieve, but about why, and how, and what the results will be when you achieve it. I'm talking about communicating until the message sinks into the very muscular fibers of your heart, making your heart beat with yearning for it. And then, share it some more, until your voice hurts from talking about it.

Why all this sharing? The more you share your dream, the more energy you give to your vision, and the more support you create to keep you accountable to that vision.

When you declare your goal consistently and with conviction, you'll have no time or energy left to dwell on or talk about all the crap that happened in the past. When you set your mental, emotional, physical, and spiritual energy toward the future, it propels you into that future. When you share that energy with others, it propels you with even greater power and velocity.

The only way to share that energy with others is through deliberate, purposeful communication. So focus on communication that's about the future and its possibilities. Your talk will light the jets that launch your goal into flight.

Maybe you don't know "how" your invented future will be created yet. So what? Neither did JFK. You might be thinking that of course, he was the president and could therefore command a large number of people to figure out how to achieve his goal. But you can do something similar. If you share your vision with enough "possibility" people, you'll begin to attract people who have some ideas about *how*, or at least, *how to find out how.*

The more people you share your vision with, the more likely it is you'll find others who will be eager to play a part in that vision. And in the process, you, too, will begin researching and discovering answers about *how*. How could you not?

The moon landing is an extraordinary example. But ordinary people become extraordinary by envisioning something others don't dare to dream, doing the things others aren't willing to do, and then having the patience to keep at it until they see results.

Maybe you're tempted to tell yourself that you've already blown too many chances. Maybe you're looking at everything that's gone wrong before, or you're looking at all the current circumstances stacked against you. Stop! Hit fast forward and play a new tune, starting now.

Envision the future you would want if anything were possible, and then begin living your way into it.

At the beginning, you might feel nervous. But that doesn't mean you've made the wrong choice. It is normal to be nervous when your life is about to change. What's really inspiring is when you notice a different kind of energy start to pulse through you. Soon you'll feel it infecting those around you—and it's not nervousness anymore, but a feeling of excitement about your new future.

There Are Two Sides To Every Table

Whether it was in a boardroom, at a coffee shop, or around your kitchen table, I'll bet you're familiar with the kind of depressing ending to a meeting I'm about to describe.

We had just finished a strategy session to establish some ambitious new goals, but when we completed almost everyone looked doubtful, cynical, or downright irritable.

Even though everyone on the board had listened politely to the new goals during the meeting, afterward it seemed nobody was buying into the possibility that we could actually accomplish them.

How quickly negativity can find supporters!

Once the grumbling began, there were plenty of people ready to join in. I heard board members nodding and agreeing as they said things to each other like, "It's not likely to happen in this economy," and "Our share in the market has done nothing but shrink over the last 36 months," and "I can't sign off on a plan that's not based in reality."

For a moment it looked as if everything we'd just put on the table was about to be swept off.

Then, a single voice of true possibility emerged from a chair on the other side of the table. The woman's voice was powerful and clear. She dared to speak of something she saw that nobody else seemed even willing to imagine. She said, if you'll allow me to paraphrase, "Gentlemen. What we need here is a *miracle result* to accomplish this unifying goal."

There was an uncomfortable pause, filled with plenty of throat clearing around the table.

She continued. "These goals are possible only if we approach them from a new mindset. We cannot grow this company as we currently see it. We need to get into a conversation about what we *can* do, as opposed to what we *cannot* do. If we could do that at this level, then perhaps we could create some magic in this business and industry."

Then, she got bold. "You all seem more comfortable with cynicism than you do with solutions. I challenge all of us to support these ideas with resources and go for a big return rather than our normal course of reasonableness."

Her words were transformative. Negativity was replaced by possibility, cynicism by imagination. Amazing what one leader can do. Amazing how leadership can arise when one person is willing to get real about possibility.

Which side of the table have you been sitting on lately? Are you grumbling with the cynics and stacking your side of the table with reams of logical, reasonable evidence for pessimism? What's the harm in considering the possibility that this bold new idea might be just as logical and reasonable as the arguments against it?

When presented with any idea that requires us to change, we tend to deceive ourselves into believing we lack ability, resources, or options. Most of us don't do this because we're dishonest or lazy. We cling to the status quo because of our internal fears. We're afraid that a change in our attitude might require some uncomfortably bold actions.

So we rationalize why there's no need to change. That's the easier, softer way.

But when we do that, we risk stagnation and even paralysis, the precursors to ultimate failure. In the face of that potential failure, what harm is there in simply asking the *what if* questions?

What if more were possible? What if we could accomplish this dream? What if we simply considered what we would need to do to make this happen?

When you allow yourself to see possibilities, it's easier to see the steps to achieving them, and once you see those steps, it's much easier to actually take them. If you're dealing in the possible, your actions will have more power and decisiveness behind them than if you're mired in uncertainty and fear.

The power of saying yes to "what if" is the power of turning ideas into actions and actions into results.

I'll admit that I do take the duck-and-cover attitude from time to time. But I find that the more vigilant I am about not letting fear take over clear thinking, the more I can see beyond my current limiting viewpoint. Being a leader involves seeing beyond what has been done before. The leadership that is open to considering new possibilities is the leadership that can lead to achieving new realities.

Walt Disney was another leader with a talent for envisioning something never before considered and then moving his life in the direction of that vision. Disneyland was once just a small orange grove, but Walt imagined something else. He instead saw a magic kingdom, where parents and children could play together amid a fantasy of moon rockets and castles, flying elephants and giant teacups, mountains and rivers and waterfalls.

He then shared this dream with anyone who would listen. It wasn't easy. Disney once said, "I could never convince the financiers that Disneyland was feasible, because dreams offer too little collateral."

He ultimately agreed to create a weekly television show for ABC in return for funding, which also allowed him to capture the imagination of the American public and garner more support. Walt shared his idea until it took hold of so many people there was no turning back.

I challenge you as a leader to venture into the land of the unbelievable. Then make your powerful declaration that triggers possibility. Soon the unbelievable has become believable because *you said it was.*

The impossible becomes possible when you line up every cell in your body toward that endeavor. Maintaining long-term faith in your vision requires the strength to continuously renew your conviction in the face of the naysayers.

They will prove to you that it's always easier to come up with reasons *why not* than with reasons *why.* But you will prove to them that it's not always better to do that.

Sure, some new ideas can actually be stupid. But those ideas are often motivated by greed without meaningful purpose, or they're empty dreams without the will to commit to the hard work of research, planning, implementation, and follow-through. If you have an idea that you truly believe in, and you're willing to commit to action from beginning to end, then you need not concern yourself with limitations.

Ironically, the ability to turn the unbelievable into reality is even more important in tough economic times. It is precisely when times are tough that we most need new thinking. Hard times are the best times to throw out old ideas and embrace creativity and innovation. When the gloom descends on the marketplace it is exactly the time for optimists to step forward with what-if ideas.

Chances are you've already spent plenty of time evaluating and defining "what's wrong." If so, it's time to solve "what's wrong" by asking a new question: "What's working?"

Get Real

The next time you're in a meeting and you get the sinking feeling that the goals of your boss or employees, team members or partners, family or friends are "unrealistic," pause and ask yourself:

Which side of the table am I sitting on? Am I sitting on the "this can't be done" side, or the "what if we could" side?

There's no need to determine whether either of you is right or wrong. Just give yourself permission to experiment with that second question, "What if we could?"

If you have a tablet or computer open in front of you, write the question down: "What is working?" As you and the others at the table talk, listen for possible answers to that question. Let the energy build. With those insights in hand, at the end of the meeting, you will experience a shift in consciousness that is more solution oriented. Once that shift has occurred then you can begin to ask a great leader's question, "What's next?"

———————————

7

Create Something from Nothing

A Blank Slate

We often hear people say things like, "I'm a creative person," or "I do creative work." We assume that they are designers or artists.

But the truth is that effective leadership of any kind requires creativity. So it's good to know how your own creativity is best accessed and applied.

When you want to create something, you must learn to start with nothing. Nothing is the launching pad.

Most people never realize that, which is why they falsely conclude that they are not creative, as if they have a personality deficit. But we are all innately creative. We just don't know the value of starting from nothing.

Sure, it's possible to create something from something else, but it won't be something new. Instead, it will be a reiteration, a variation, a re-creation—of what came before.

To create something new, different and unique requires the ability to let go of *everything* and get back to *nothing*. Turning nothing into something is the ultimate act of creation.

All creativity starts with one thing: a thought. That thought, too, comes from nothing—a blank slate on which you can draw anything. If you want to create something, you must open your mind to nothing.

So what am I talking about? Maybe you want to write a book, so you start with a blank page. Maybe you want to build a new home, so you begin with a cleared piece of ground. Maybe you want to increase sales in your department, so you start a new client relationship where before there was none.

If you're feeling bold, maybe you want to create a new product or service. That means asking yourself, "What need or want exists in the world that has never before been considered or fulfilled?"

What is the value of nothing?

When we feel frustrated with stalled ideas or lagging results, part of the problem is thinking that whatever we want to accomplish must start with something we already know or already have. That's a false assumption. Invariably, the leaders I coach get the best results when they set aside notions of what they or others have done in the past. Those leaders instead pull the lid off, leaving their minds wide open to the thing that has never before occurred to them, allowing a new vision to float in.

Though this may sound like magic at first, like pulling a rabbit out of a hat, if you think about it, there's nothing more real or basic than starting with nothing.

When you start with a blank slate, you gain freedom, because you no longer *rely on* the people or ideas that came before. When you start with a blank slate, accountability is built in, because you no longer *blame* the people or ideas that came before. You are responsible for your own results. That can be scary, but it's also empowering, because no one has a preconceived notion of what these never-before results will look like.

Here comes the tricky part:

Even if everything in your life, professional and personal, is going well, if you want to keep going strong, you'll still want to engage in thinking about *nothing*. *Nothing thinking* will help you keep everything you do fresh and powerful. It keeps you on your toes when the curtains of life open on a new show every night.

Have you ever been in a relationship, or known one, in which everything was going well, yet the couple still ended up going their separate ways?

So what happened? Boredom? Disenchantment? Stagnation?

Maybe so, but where did that come from? We can't always be sure because romance can't be treated like a formula. However, my guess is that somewhere along the way someone stopped coming from nothing.

If you say the words she once loved to hear, or touch her the way that once drove her wild, or do the same things together you've always done—then if you were happy then, you'll be happy now, right?

Wrong. That's a recipe for failure. Your needs and hers, your wants and hers, will shift throughout a lifetime.

If you aren't willing to see that person with fresh eyes every day, and if you aren't alert to changes in the relationship, or if you aren't willing to regularly consider new mutual goals—someone's likely to get tired of the status quo.

The same is true in all areas of our lives, especially business.

I often talk to people who work hard, never varying, never wavering, for years on end. These are people who seem to be waiting for wealth to arrive in their bank account as a reward for all their years of labor. But unless they've signed a contract that says doing the same things they've always done will result in new, untold wealth, they might just as well wait to win the lottery.

Doing the same old thing, no matter how hard you work at it, will most likely yield the same old results.

Starting with nothing is the way out of that kind of stagnation. And even though it will feel like a risk, it's the only gamble that ever changes anything. Many of the wealthiest people I know had nothing when they began. Many of the happiest people I know grew their joy from nothing.

Those people didn't just sit atop the something they created and call it a day, either. Instead they kept asking, "What next?" And the answer never started with, "Well, let's see what we did before..."

Some people who claim they want to create something new, make the mistake of wanting it to succeed instantly: something from nothing...right now! This get rich quick mentality is not about creating something *from* nothing, it's about expecting something *for* nothing.

Creating something new requires the application of thought and action. If you don't apply much thought or action, you can expect proportional results of—not much. It's tempting to look for the easy way, but if you waste time trying to brainstorm the easy idea, and then waste more time trying to make it happen, and then repeat that effort over and over again, you'll learn that the "easy way" can be the hardest way of all.

That may be why many of us have been struggling with the new "tough" economy. The economic bubble has burst in a way that has created a new global reality. Things used to be easier; now they're not. Yet many people keep acting the way they used to act, in hopes they'll achieve the results they used to achieve.

Our economy cannot return to the reality denying, spend-more-to-make-more, entitled consumer-fest it was. If you try to plot ways to make that happen, you're back to trying to create something from something. Nothing new will come of that. Things are different now. Like it or not, if you want to make it in a "tough" economy, you need to be ready with some "tough" new thinking, "tough" new ideas, and "tough" new action.

Opening yourself to nothing doesn't mean closing your eyes to reality. Rather, to create a vision from nothing, we must close our eyes for a moment and be ready to see things with a fresh perspective when we open them. If you do that right now, when you open your eyes, you may notice that the world has changed since the last time you took a good hard look. The ability to create something from nothing will allow you to not only see the way the world has changed, but to see the way it might change in future. With that in mind, you may glimpse an idea of how you can be part of that change... for the better.

I work with people and companies to help them get aligned with the idea of nothing. We don't just start from scratch. We start *before* scratch, so that often even the raw ingredients aren't yet on the table. I know that if leaders hold on to the "we already have something, so let's work with that" way of behaving, then they're liable to find themselves waiting a very long time for results.

Waiting is death to a progressive company or person.

When artists create, they take many classes to learn their craft. But they also know the importance of spending time experimenting without regard to rules, traditions, or known forms. Sometimes they sit down to paint or sculpt or carve, with absolutely no idea what they want to work on today.

I encourage you to slide your brush over a fresh canvas. Go ahead and dare to ask yourself some radical questions, like: what if I approach my business, or my social life, or my personal life, from an entirely new perspective? What if I'm willing to try something I've never considered before?

You may find a part of yourself you never knew existed, a part you've always denied, a part that can carry you to new heights. You may receive the kind of gift that's so inspiring it prompts you to celebrate this moment of clarity as a new day of birth.

Whatever you do in response to your new vision, it's important to keep moving toward that vision, and after you achieve it, erase the slate and envision something new. Remind yourself at each new start that any great thing that has ever occurred began from NO-thing. Where there is NO-thing, there can one day be SOME-thing. When you understand this, you will be a true creator, and true creativity is the driver of all success.

The Value Of Nothing

Not only do we create from nothing, but also sometimes we need to sit back and do nothing at all, without any agenda or expectation.

One time I was just sitting in a chair with a blank look on my face, and a friend asked, "What are you doing?" I replied, "I'm doing nothing."

This may sound lazy. But for purpose-driven people like me, sometimes it can be the hardest work of all. It can also be the most rewarding.

Great leaders understand the difference between being lazy and doing nothing. Some people are so frozen by indecision that doing nothing would only add to the suffering of inaction. If you're lazy, or a procrastinator, this section is not for you. I'm addressing those of you who are purpose-driven or obsessive. You know who you are: you talk fast and never sit still, you're fiery and bold, you have an answer to everything and you're usually sure you're right. You don't think much before you jump onto the next project, into the river, or out of the plane—sometimes you're a PITA (pain in the ass.) If that's you, stick with me.

As someone who tends to remain in constant motion, I've discovered that doing nothing is a lot more useful than it sounds. It not only recharges my batteries, it also allows me the space to create the blank slate I've been talking about. I make a point of setting aside time to do nothing when there's something big at stake. I'm talking about stillness, silence, and surrender. Some call this prayer, but I don't want to muddy the waters here. When I say I do nothing, I mean *nothing.*

Sometimes I do nothing because I have no idea what to do. Have you ever watched somebody who has no idea what to do, who then starts to do a lot of random, useless things one after another? That kind of directionless flailing is painful to watch.

I've learned that not knowing is OK. Not knowing always precedes knowing. When I'm doing nothing, I surrender to not knowing, which opens me to the possibility of knowing. So, when I do nothing, I'm doing everything. I'm preparing my blank slate for any and all possibilities.

This may seem to fly in the face of my overall leadership philosophy. I typically believe that leaders are people of action. But when you aren't clear on your objective, or the best path to that objective, the best action you can take is no action. At those times, I invite you to block off some time to sit still and do *nada.*

Should you think during that time? If you want. This is your nothing, not mine. Like I said, I'm not necessarily talking about meditation. So do your own form of nothing:

think about your life and the direction you want to go, or let your mind wander, or just let your mind go blank. Go to the beach, stare at the waves, and just breathe.

The world is moving at warp speed and so are you. So sitting still is actually a great way to shift energy and shake things up. You're creating the space for your inner wisdom and intuition to reveal their purpose to you, or for the future to give hints of what it wants from you.

I've received some of my best insights while doing nothing. Often it's only by doing nothing now that I know what action to take tomorrow.

When you stop long enough to hear the quiet voice inside of you, you might be amazed at how much it knows about who you are, what you need, and your best path to succeed. The more often you do this, the better you'll get to know yourself.

Great leaders know themselves. That means they know when to do something and when to do nothing. When they do take action, it's targeted and decisive.

Doing nothing requires me to let go of some of my ingrained beliefs. I have to loosen up on the puritanical work ethic that is, for better or worse, America's psychic inheritance.

For example, I have an office loft away from home, but sometimes I think I should dispense with this luxury and work at home. Then I remind myself that my loft is not a luxury, but a sanctuary. The reason for my internal struggle is this: when I'm in the loft, I often do nothing. Sometimes I embellish stories about what I do at the loft, just to prove to myself that I'm highly productive. The truth is, I've come up with many great ideas, solutions, and plans during or after a do-nothing session in my loft.

If you're a purpose-driven person, don't feel defensive or worried about doing nothing. It will serve you.

This American attachment to the virtue of busy-ness can be even harder to overcome when you're dealing with other people. When you see someone sitting still who's supposed to be working with you, it's easy to become suspicious. Is she taking advantage of me? Is she procrastinating? Indeed, we've run into such people before and we will again, but hyper-vigilance won't prevent that. When you catch someone doing nothing, don't be quick to judge. Let their results be your guide.

When you're working with partners based on mutual agreement, it's un-empowering to monitor their minutes like a babysitter. The question isn't how they spend their time, but whether they achieve results. Sometimes optimal results require down time.

In my study of great spiritual leaders, I've found that almost all of them have, or have had, a practice of retreat. When they've wanted to gain clarity on what to do next, they've first stopped and done nothing. As Mahatma Gandhi once said, "I have so much to accomplish today that I must meditate for two hours instead of one." Gandhi's times of stillness gave him the answers he needed to help free a nation.

Aren't you curious to discover what you can do, if you first stop and do nothing?

Get Real

If you're an active person in both body and mind, it may take some effort for you to get into that stillness of mind that precedes the productive process of envisioning ideas. You may need to schedule time to meditate or take yoga, walk or hike, listen to music or bake. Do whatever you need to do to free your mind from its usual thoughts and patterns.

When you're ready to try some full-on nothing, pull out your calendar and schedule five minutes to an hour of time and label it: "Do nothing." During that time, don't force the ideas, just relax and embrace nothingness. Once you get to a place where your mind is empty of all that has gone before, ask yourself, "If I could do anything at all, what would it be?" This question might refer to a problem you've been working on, or it might simply be an openness to whatever's next for you.

Still not sure you can still your mind and create from nothing? Then try this thought experiment: imagine that your accomplishments, experience, education, opinion have all ceased to exist. Now, how would you make 10 dollars this week? Got an idea? OK, now how could you manifest 100 dollars this week? Have you wrapped your brain around that idea? OK, now take it to the next level: what can you do this week to put events in motion that would bring 10,000 dollars your way by week's end?

When your do-nothing session is over, if you haven't come up with any ideas yet, don't worry. You may need more practice to relax and let go. Or the ideas may arrive later, long after the down time is over. On the other hand, if you find yourself with a new idea at the end of your down time, don't just sit there. Go for it!

8

If You Want to Succeed, Be Willing To Fail

Failure Is A Reality

Successful people fail. In fact, the most highly successful people tally up more failures than others.

They don't merely face setbacks, or overcome obstacles, or deal with challenges—they actually fail.

But failing does not make them *failures*. Quite the opposite.

When you fail at something along the way, it doesn't mean that you don't have what it takes. In fact, it doesn't mean anything. You had a goal or objective, and you didn't meet it. That's all it means.

Our mistakes don't define whether or not we are successes or failures. It is *how we deal with our mistakes* that matters.

When I fail to achieve a goal, it's tempting to wax on about all the reasons why I didn't make it. Many people do this. Certainly, it can be useful to look at everything that happened along the way, so I can determine what elements contributed to the failure, and what different elements might

to success. But if I want success in the future, then
ing responsibility for my role in the failures along the
way must be part of the equation. Bemoaning *what happened
to me* is not nearly as important as being accountable for the
actions I took or failed to take. Accountability is a habit of
leadership. Making excuses is not.

On the other hand, it's counterproductive to rehash
mistakes over and over, fueling regret over the past, wishful
thinking about what might have been, or doubt about the
future. Beating yourself up diminishes the very self-esteem
you'll need to get back on track. It also diminishes the esteem
others hold for you. You might think they'll appreciate your
humility but it's more likely that they'll see you as self-pitying,
attention seeking, or time wasting.

A rapid admission of responsibility, an apology, and a
new plan are all you need to wipe the slate clean and get back
into action.

The best way to get back onto the path of success after a
failure is to quickly assess the damage, commit to a new
course of action, and move on.

Although many people feel guilty when they fail, in
public they tend to deflect attention from their responsibility
by downplaying it or talking around it. They don't use words
like "failure" or "mistake" or "apology." Instead they talk
about regretting "what happened," or they explain all the
extenuating circumstances over which they had no control.
I've never understood that. I think it becomes harder for
everyone to move on when we don't call it like it is.

Here's how I see it: either I made my goal or I didn't, either I won or lost, either I succeeded or failed.

Even some leaders who are willing to face failure head-on often begin their discussion of a failure by listing the reasons why something didn't work. I want to be clear here: evaluating "why" in terms of recognizing what actions did or didn't work is a useful exercise, but evaluating "why" in terms of blaming other people, external circumstances, or bad luck is typically a waste of time.

Allow me to confirm something you already know: most people you work with won't care why you didn't meet your objective. They'll just want to know what you're going to do to fix it, and how you plan to improve your approach in the future.

Everyone makes mistakes every day, and most people will accept that if you're up front with them. What they won't accept is endless rationalizations or lies. You might think you won't get caught at that game, but the potential price is not worth the risk. Whether in business or the arts, sports or hobbies, family or friendship—almost all of our goals involve and affect our relationships, and relationships are built on trust. You will build more trust with others if you can admit to mistakes quickly and cleanly, without excuses, and then identify how you plan to move on to success.

I can honor my own integrity when I can own up to the fact that I did not complete the last goal, and give reasonable assurances of what I plan to do to complete the next goal.

Sure I fear failure sometimes, and I feel bad when it happens. But facing failure is facing reality. If I call a failure a failure, rather than focusing my attention on what a terrible person I think I am, or what I can do to distract you from seeing what a terrible person I think I am—I can instead focus my attention on how to use this "failure" as a growth tool.

Now let's look at a more radical possibility: the possibility that leaders actually thrive on failure. Great leaders all eventually learn what Thomas Watson of IBM said: "If you want to succeed more, fail more."

Personally, I like feeling the heat of failure in my very soul. I don't want off the hook. I don't want to ask my friends to comfort me and tell me it wasn't as bad as I think it was. To me, that would be like telling them that I'm unable to handle my weaknesses. When I accept the experience of embracing my dying goal as it goes down in flames, I find it easier to learn and grow and come out the other side laughing like a clown.

Don't deny failure. Embrace it as if it were your greatest teacher.

From my greatest failures have come my greatest lessons. As long as I'm learning lessons, I'm on the road to success. When I acknowledge failure and learn from it, it's easier to commit not to repeat it.

This isn't just about putting a positive spin on things. Humans really do learn how to do things the right way by first doing them the wrong way. Watch a baby learn to walk. Struggle yourself in a strange new country, speaking a language that's new to you. You can only learn from your mistakes.

Children have less of a problem dealing with this than we do. They fail all day every day and don't think much about it.

The great psychologist Dr. Thomas Szasz put it this way: "Every act of conscious learning requires the willingness to suffer an injury to one's self-esteem. That is why young children, before they are aware of their own self-importance, learn so easily."

The best leaders I advise have learned to put the success of the team way ahead of their own self-importance.

When you truly look at failure as a learning experience, you'll see that the key to success is found in failing. I'm not suggesting you study failure as a way of life, but rather that you allow yourself to do what scientists do, and see everything you engage in as an experiment.

You're either discovering what to do, or what not to do—that's it. There's no need to blame anyone in that. Your actions, whether they succeed or fail, are only the path that takes you closer to the goal.

When we pursue success without negative self-judgment or defensiveness, we see both the progress and the mistakes as necessary materials for paving the road to success. Sometimes the mistakes lead to tough times, but when you learn to see the tough times as gifts, they will open their secrets to you.

The Best of Us Are Failures

Most of the people I mentor have a hard time making a mistake. I can identify with them. Many times in my life or business dealings I've had that same fear of making wrong decisions. When a bold choice confronted me, my mind started churning on all the things that could go wrong. This kind of thinking used to freeze me up like a winter pond.

But the ice broke when I finally realized that there's no way to know if a decision is good or bad until after you make it. What if I could see both possibilities as steps toward success? What if I could give myself the freedom to make a mistake? I realized I would be more willing to make the bold moves that lead to invention and innovation—true watchwords of success.

If your choice turns out to be right, you take a step forward. If your choice turns out to be wrong, it informs your next choice—and still, you take a step forward. If you don't give yourself the freedom to fail, you take no steps forward at all; you just stand there, indecisive and afraid. And voilà, your fear of failure becomes failure by default.

Sometimes all the time we spend trying to decide something becomes failure in and of itself. Inaction is failure. And tentative, uncommitted action can also lead to failure.

Wise men and women can help us avoid some mistakes by sharing what they've learned. But they can also be examples: if you listen to them you'll notice that most of what they learned they learned by making mistakes. Some of that mistake making you'll have to do for yourself. Unless you only want to achieve what they have already achieved, and why waste time on that?

It's ironic isn't it? Often the fear of messing up is what makes us mess up. Why? When we've set up an inner judge to stare over our shoulder, watching and waiting for us to mess up, we become nervously ineffective. When that internal judge promises to label us a failure for each mistake, our movements become constrained. We are no longer freewheeling and creative. We are no longer at our best. Our mind expends so much energy trying to guess how not to screw up that it has little energy left to imagine the possible actions that would lead to success.

Leaders are most likely to turn to me for coaching when they're struggling with a problem, a transition, or a tough decision. Sometimes their choices involve risking tremendous amounts of money, respected reputations, or important relationships. I have compassion for people facing these kinds of choices. Yet, I often see leaders put themselves through unnecessary suffering over the process, even when they can't possibly predict the outcome either way.

I had the privilege of interviewing Bill Farley, the former CEO of Jordache and Fruit of the Loom, and I took the opportunity to ask him what he thought set him apart from the hordes of businessmen who never made it to the top. His answer was simple: "My willingness to make the tough decisions."

He didn't agonize or let himself get paralyzed with the fear of failure.

After you've done your due diligence and researched all the pros and cons of the choices before you, it's time to either listen to your gut, or just put your finger on the map and go. Don't waste your time and the time of others. Get bold, make a move, and watch what grows.

If you don't see success growing outside you, stop and take a look inside yourself. That's where the growth will happen, if you're willing to accept failure, learn from it, and move on to the next tough choice.

One day each of us is going to die, and most of us will have a tombstone, or at least a eulogy or obituary. Imagine for a second that yours will read one of two ways:

"…a nice person who never made a mistake."

OR

"…a true leader who inspired us all by living courageously."

Get Real

What decision are you avoiding right now? If you haven't researched the pros and cons, schedule yourself half a day this week, or an hour each night, to do that. If you've already researched the pros and cons, write them down on a sheet of paper. Read through that list, and then rip it up or ball it up and throw it in the trash. Close your eyes and envision an end result for each choice. Don't try to see all the results of each choice. Just pick one clear image for each. Now, open your eyes and ask yourself, "What choice do I trust in my gut?" Write down the answer. There's your decision. Now go talk to whomever you need to talk to, do whatever you need to do, or schedule whatever you need to schedule so that you can share your decision with someone else in the world and start making it real.

9

No More Pretending...
Get Real!

A Commitment to Authenticity

I was at a speaking engagement on the East Coast when, out of the blue, I began to question the difference between positive thinking and intelligence. There was something magical about considering the two concepts side-by-side.

It's easy to see that positive thinking has the power to benefit almost everyone; it rarely hurts to engage in affirming, encouraging, optimistic thoughts, does it? At the very least, adopting a positive attitude will likely be of more service to more people than choosing to be cynical.

However, I've known some people who've focused more on having a positive attitude than developing intelligence. By intelligence I mean our capacity for learning, reasoning, and understanding.

I remember once going to work with a bad head cold. You know the kind: red eyes, runny nose, fever, all of which I tried to minimize with a plastic smile. People would ask, "How are you feeling?" I'd instinctively reply something along the lines of, "I'm feeling better all the time," or "Don't worry about me."

Telling someone I felt fine when I actually felt like hell almost had a higher yuck factor than the cold itself. Everyone knew I felt like crap. I looked terrible. I just wasn't being authentic. Yet I was so afraid of the stigma of negative thinking that I wouldn't allow myself to get real.

I don't know when my fear of the truth began. Maybe it was a Peter Lowe seminar I did in the 1990s. Wherever it happened, I learned to be fairly automatic about always saying, "I'm great!" without really being present with the truth.

I'm sure I'm not the only one who has ever converted to this mindless optimism. I've seen the plastic smiles on clients who've said the same thing to me, when it was clear they were hanging on the edge and afraid to admit it. As if naming what they were really feeling would give it power over them, like some sort of demon.

Having said that, let's introduce intelligent thinking as an alternative to the false positive. That week when I was sick, it would have been more intelligent to cop to the fact that something funky was running out of my nose, my body ached, my thoughts were fuzzy—and that all this was evidence that I was in dire need of rest. What terrible thing did I think was going to happen if I came out and admitted the truth: "I don't feel great." If I had done that, it's not as if all my positive options would have gone away. In fact, this would have been a perfect opportunity to add a more reality-based optimism to the equation. I could have added, "I'm going to take some vitamin C," or, "I'm going to go home early and get some rest," or even, "I feel terrible today, but I'm taking care of myself and I believe I can lick this thing by tomorrow."

Responding with a presence of mind that reflects an intelligent assessment of the facts rather than mindless, knee-jerk positive thinking is an authentic place to come from. When we get real about where we are at the moment, we lay the groundwork to seek the solutions and ideas we need to create real results in the future.

The "I'm fine" answer has become our collective "auto-response" to the ubiquitous "How are you?" question. My challenge to you is this: the next time you're tempted to string together a group of words just because they're the expected response, or to put forth a positive but unrealistic front just because you fear that everything will go south if you don't, instead try speaking the truth and moving on. The long-term results will astound you. They've astounded me.

The truth is a gift to people. It inspires trust. You become someone people can count on to be real and even trustworthy. That is no small thing in our highly interconnected world today.

Programs that offer visualization philosophies can go a long way in initiating our journey toward living beautiful lives. They can help us envision and plan a future from nothing. However, it's important that we not lose touch with reality along the way.

My head cold is just one simple example. We all face moments when we have an opportunity to share with others how things are going with our work, our relationships, or any of our endeavors. And at one time or another we all say things are fine when they're anything but. Once you can "own" your runny nose, you can begin to heal more quickly than if you deny it. You cannot leave a place that you have never been: if you don't admit the undesirable place where you stand, how can you figure out a way to hightail it out of there? Getting real with where you are in your life empowers you to see what it is you want to create, and to envision the steps you need to take to get there.

As opposed to playing it "cool," being authentic allows you to create more real connections with others. You'll feel better about yourself, and people will feel much closer to you. When you start from that place, it's much easier to roll up your sleeves together and make great things happen.

Truth-telling

Imagine what the world would be like if we all only opened our mouths to tell the truth. Imagine if you not only told the truth to others, but also first insisted on being honest with yourself. Imagine you didn't just casually accept the value of honesty, but considered it a path to a higher calling, because you believed that knowing your authentic self was a first step to knowing what you wanted, which was a first step to success.

That's what I vowed to do many years back when I still had a J-O-B: Tell the truth.

I can still remember the aching pit that would open up deep in my stomach as I made the drive to work each day. I was a banker, and I liked my work. Rather, I liked what I believed my work should be. What I didn't like were all the games people played at work: office politics, leveraging, one-upmanship, backstabbing, and brown-nosing just to name a few. It seemed like a prerequisite to working in corporate America back then and still seems so today.

I disliked the pretension and posturing; it soon felt like glue was sticking to every surface in the office, including my own skin. I'm sure I wasn't the only one who hated it. People would sit in meetings with plastic smiles on their faces, pretending to appreciate what the boss was saying, and heads nodding up and down like bobble-head dogs. We were yes-men and yes-women. Robots.

It took me a while to realize that I could never win at these games, because the person sitting in my chair playing them was no longer me.

It turned out that there was a good side to this unnatural, unpleasant feeling. It was something like what Napoleon Hill described as "inspirational dissatisfaction." My discomfort opened up a new kind of exploration for me.

I began to ask myself, "If I don't want to be this robot, then who do I want to be? What do I want to achieve? And how could I present myself to the world so I can go about achieving it?"

I had become so painfully unhappy with the inauthentic approach I'd developed to survive at my job, that I decided to go the opposite way: I decided to explore the authentic side of myself.

Soon I was experimenting with *expressing* this more authentic side of myself to others. I began to think of it as a new form of assertive leadership. And maybe it was. But in practice it wasn't too complicated: I was simply being real.

My newfound goal was to show up in my life and the lives of others as an authentic being.

But before I could do that consistently I knew I had to make some bona fide shifts in my life. First, I had to learn to recognize the truth as I saw it, and to ask myself to identify that truth in every situation. Then I had to be willing to speak that truth to others.

Soon after I made that shift, I was sitting in a strategic planning meeting at my company. I remember a staff member was sitting in on the meeting who I felt had no place there. So I came right out and said so, clearly and simply, "Chris shouldn't be here. He needs to leave."

If you guessed that this created an uncomfortable moment or two in that meeting, you're right. But, as uncomfortable as it was, Chris did gather up his pad and pen and leave. And, despite the tension, I felt certain that it was a move in the right direction.

From then on, the notion of agreeing with something just because everyone else did—or rather, because no one else said anything—was no longer going to work for me. Other people in the meeting agreed that I'd made an integral choice.

That simple moment held a revelation. I realized that a significant and appropriate way of gaining the respect of others is to tell the truth, especially when it's not an easy truth to tell. From that day forward, I began to speak the truth, not with any underlying motive, but simply because it was the truth.

Each of us has our own perception of truth, and someone else's view of the world may not always line up with your view or mine. What remains important is that we speak our own truth and value it in others.

Your truth is derived from your own perceptions, experiences, and intuitive processes. It's also important to remember that your perception of the truth can shift in an instant based upon every new piece of information you gather.

The moment you think you're certain of a thing, you create boundaries that impede learning. The truth may be changeable, but seeking it is a process that each of us must embark on for ourselves.

What's most important is that, when you discover your truth, you can then live and breathe it. When you "walk your talk," a whole new realm of possibility will open up for you.

Being Wrong Is Sometimes Right

When I was in the fifth grade, I often raised my hand in class. I wanted the teacher to be proud of me and the other kids to like me. I remember thinking, "Call on me! Please, please, please! I think I know the answer!" I wanted to have an answer to everything. Sometimes my hand was in the air, *even when I wasn't sure I knew the answer.* It didn't really matter at that age whether I was wrong or right, *I just wanted to play.*

However, as time went on, I saw that the kids with the right answers were the ones being praised for being "smart." I remember the teacher asking: "Who has the right answer?" and beaming at that boy or girl and saying, "That's right!"

Over time, my hand was not as quick to dart into the air.

I was no longer happy to simply play along in the game of question and answer. I started to worry about having the right answer.

It starts early, doesn't it? And if we're not careful, the fear of being wrong can stifle us for a lifetime.

When was the last time you saw a game show? These days there can be millions of dollars riding on the right answer. "If you can answer this last triple bonus question, you'll win 50 million dollars and live happily ever after!" But, you can imagine yourself in the hot seat, sweating, thinking, "If I'm wrong the audience will groan, and my dreams will vanish, and for the rest of my life everyone will remember this as the moment I officially became a loser."

In modern society, teachers, parents, and peers constantly reward us for being right. Teachers praise us for getting the right answer, parents praise us for getting the right grades and winning the right competitions, peers praise us for saying the right things and wearing the right clothes—the cool things, the hot clothes. We're trained to think that knowing is better than not knowing.

Think about the last time you knew the right answer. How did it feel? Now think about the last time you opened your mouth and said something no one else agreed with. How did that feel? Face it, in America at least, most of us feel like we need to be right.

But if we want to become effective, authentic leaders, we must begin to retrain ourselves. The old childhood programming won't serve us any longer. It's still fun to be right, but we have to understand that what may seem like a "wrong" answer may turn out to be a good answer anyway. Sometimes we need to discover and eliminate all the wrong answers before we can find the right one. And, most important of all, sometimes there is no right or wrong answer—only the possibilities we imagine and what we make of them.

In leadership, we allow all answers to have space in our head and on the table. Our love of the truth replaces the need to be right. Our relationship to reality becomes stronger. We learn to get real.

Now we're using everything that we discover along the way as an opportunity to learn and grow. We're creating a culture in which everyone on our team is encouraged to seek solutions, even when we're not sure of the right answer—*especially* when we're not sure of the right answer.

I suspect some of you may have a panicked ego shouting in your head right now, "Is this leadership nut telling me I should start *trying* to be wrong?"

No, I'm not asking you to go out of your way to be wrong. I'm asking you to let go of the idea that being sure of the right answer is the most critical component to success. I'm asking you to be creative and innovative—which means testing out new answers that have not yet been proven.

If you want to give the world something new and exciting, the best way to start is with the attitude, "I have no idea how to make this happen yet, what if we wanted to _____? Any ideas?" And remember, often the best ideas don't seem that way at first. Often they're the dumb ones, the crazy ones, the "I can't believe it" ones…and, I dare say, the "wrong" ones.

I recently led a strategic team planning session for a mid-level corporate team. I asked, "What is most unique about our product?"

There were 22 people in the room, and yet the response was total silence.

I knew where the tension was coming from. I could feel it in the air, see it on their faces: "What if I don't answer accurately? I might look stupid." It took some convincing for me to pry open their mouths. I asked them to play with this, to have fun, to enjoy the game. Soon we were exploring all the possibilities, and yes, some of the ideas offered made us laugh—and sometimes those ideas were the best ones.

But I could see that they finally realized that the only way we were going to figure out what was unique about the product was to lay it all out there, right or wrong. We had a fun time, and ultimately came up with a great marketing campaign. But only after the team gave up their attachment to knowing the right answers and their fear of speaking the wrong ones.

It's not only in the team meeting where the fear of being wrong poses a problem. It's even more prevalent in a one-on-one interpersonal communication.

When two people are communicating together it can be difficult to stay committed to the process of seeking the truth. Immediately there arises the timeworn egoistic attachment to looking like we know what's right.

And that's a problem.

Because our desire to be right finds us taking the position that the other person must be wrong. That position is a difficult position to listen from. How can I learn anything from you if I already think you're wrong?

The need to look like we are right can also have us give up on our own true insights because we fear that we might be wrong. We don't want to be exposed. In the world of ego, looking good always trumps finding the truth.

But in the world of authentic leadership, finding the truth (and getting real) trumps everything; and how you come across means nothing in the long run.

I remember coaching a woman who was pretty dug in about how right she was in a disagreement she was having with her colleagues. And you know what? When she explained the situation to me, I had to agree, she was right.

The problem was that she was the only one holding that position, and it was keeping the team stuck. They weren't moving forward. As we spoke, I recalled the wisdom of a teacher of mine, and repeated her words to my client: "Would you rather be right, or would you rather be happy?"

There's always a choice. And the right answer isn't always right.

Get Real

The next time you find yourself in an idea meeting, brainstorm session, coffee meeting, workshop, seminar or any other situation where someone asks you for your thoughts, ideas, or answers, write this down on your notepad, computer, or your hand before you start the meeting: "Forget right. Have fun." Then, the next time it's your turn to speak, or the next time there's a long pause, search your gut—that's right, not your mind, just your gut—for one sentence on the topic at hand. Write it down if it helps. Then open your mouth and speak that one sentence, loud and clear.

If you're satisfied, sit back, relax and enjoy the ride. If you're still searching for the right answer and/or worried about what everyone is going to think, then repeat the above steps until you start having fun.

10

Connect with God and Follow Your Gut

When I was in my twenties, I had an experience that taught me self-reliance.

It wasn't just the kind of self-reliance that says, "I can take care of myself." It was a kind of reliance that said, "I trust myself to know who I am and know what's best for me."

First: I nearly died, and while lying in the hospital, I was put in touch with the Lord—the spirit within and its connection to everything. Then: I had a profound opening to make a choice about how to live the rest of my life. And because, during the "dying" process, I'd discovered myself as part of something greater, I knew my choice had to reflect that greatness.

Ever since then, staying attuned to Spirit has helped me make better choices.

Sometimes it's difficult to maintain an internal compass that points to your own true north when so many other people and external forces are pushing to convince you that north is in a different direction. Some people are so addicted to catering to social pressures that they wouldn't know true north if it hit them over the head with an iceberg.

Some people will tell you the truth as they see it, but that doesn't mean it's the truth for you. And some others are outright lying, trying to point you in a direction that benefits them, without any interest in its effects on you.

The bottom line is, while it's helpful to surround yourself with supporters interested in relationships of mutual service, ultimately the best person to rely on when you make choices—is you.

To make choices in alignment with your true north will require you to become intimately familiar with yourself: who you are, what your purpose is, and how you can fulfill your potential. Then, when you find yourself struggling with a decision, your question will be, "In what way will this or that choice serve me in fulfilling my purpose in this world as I see it?"

With that, I'll share with you how I met me. But allow me to be clear about something first: I don't believe you need a near-death experience to connect with spirit, only a willingness to see through the distractions that stand between your thoughts about the way things are and the way things actually are. As for me, I wasn't able to see the importance of that until I received a swift kick in my sense of immortality.

When I was in my late twenties, like many other people in that time of life, I lived as if I were indestructible. That's not to say I was happy. As I've told you, I worked long hours at a high-paying job I didn't much like, among colleagues whose values I didn't share.

After work I often drank four or five beers a night with clients, putting on an agreeable face that didn't match my insides. I already owned substantial private property, which seemed a mark of success, yet I was completely stressed out.

I dealt with the stress by spending long hours at the gym, until I almost achieved a bodybuilder's proportions. Of course, that only stressed my body more. Between the long work hours, long workouts, long nights of drinking, little sleep, and, most important of all, the dishonesty required for me to pretend to myself and everyone that this was the life I wanted: it was only a matter of time before something had to give. And it did.

As I recounted in my book *Learning to Believe the Unbelievable*, one day while I was working out in the gym, I felt a sharp pain in my left bicep. I blew it off, telling myself I was in fantastic shape and it was probably nothing more than a pulled muscle. A few nights later I was having dinner with my brother and his wife, when my sister-in-law said, "Your arm is purple. What's wrong with it?"

"I don't know," I said. "I might have torn a muscle." But deep down I knew a torn muscle wouldn't have turned my entire upper arm a ghastly purple, or made that arm feel so weak. The truth was I was scared to death to go to a doctor and hear bad news.

But when my sister-in-law said, "That looks terrible. You have to go see a doctor," the look on her face scared the other scared right out of me.

That night I went to the emergency room. When the admitting nurse saw my arm, she rushed to grab a doctor, and when the doctor saw it he said, "Don't move. Don't go to the bathroom. Don't even hiccup." Their faces gave away their obvious effort to appear calm and not alarm me, which told me that I had reason to be afraid.

Tests showed I had an occlusion in a major vein that ran through my bicep. That is, I had a blood clot several inches long. There was a danger of the clot traveling to my lungs, which could easily have killed me. So doctors immediately began a drug treatment to dissolve the clot. Unfortunately, I was one of a small percentage of people who have an allergic reaction to the drug prescribed. It happened quickly. One moment I was scared but hopeful the treatment would work, the next moment my body turned cold and clammy, and everything began to move in slow motion. I could feel myself leaving my body.

At that moment, I wasn't frightened anymore. Passing from life to death felt as natural as walking across a room. I didn't feel that something terrible was happening, simply that I was doing something I hadn't yet done. That's all. Doctors later confirmed that in those moments my heart stopped and I died.

I've since heard stories from many others who've had near-death experiences, and my experience didn't fit any of the stereotypes. That may be because of the difficulty of using language to describe something for which there is no language. Not long after it happened to me, I went to a conference on near-death experiences, but when I couldn't relate to the stories others were telling, I left.

It has taken me nearly 20 years to find words I felt comfortable using to talk about my temporary death, and last year I spoke publicly about it at the annual convention of the Near-Death Experience Association.

For our purposes here, suffice it to say I left my body, but there was no tunnel or white light, just a sense of becoming one with everything, and a feeling that this was a normal experience, one I'd had before. And something came over me while I was gone: a knowing that had always been within me, which I'd never known that I knew.

A doctor administered another drug that brought me back, and when I came back I brought my new sense of knowing back with me. It wasn't specific, but it permeated my mind, body, soul. I had a sense that I knew who I was and the kind of greatness I came from.

That knowledge led to a belief, which is this: I'm a leader, and while I'm here I have the power and desire to share my leadership, and to help others become leaders.

I was in no rush. It would take me another two years to grow into my new knowledge, and to leave behind that old job. But that time was now a gift, because I had a purpose. I knew that everything I did every day was now focused on moving me into alignment with that purpose.

At the conference, I shared with people that since my near-death experience, I've had similar moments many times, without having to die. I've connected deeply with Self during prayer, mountain climbing, yoga, and hiking. I believe anyone can have this experience at any time—while fly-fishing, running, or just washing dishes. It's not as much about death, as it is about embracing life without filters. It's not as much about letting go of everything, as it is about letting go of all you think you know about everything. It's not about shutting off the mind, so much as having a presence of mind. It's about being completely in the moment, and accepting life.

I spent eight days in the ICU, while they used a different blood thinner to dissolve the clot in my arm. But it didn't take eight days for me to clearly see two important things: 1) If I had died, although some would have wept at my passing, life would have gone on, and 2) My life was a gift, and that gift was mine to use in any way I chose.

My intention from then on was to live my life in a way that made a difference, but not the kind of difference I thought others would approve of. Rather, I was going to make a difference in a way that was meaningful to *me*, without reference to external standards.

I'd found my center. In the midst of an unbalanced life, I'd caught my balance.

What happened to me is a simple reminder of one of the most real truths there is: your body is going to die. There is no escaping that. So, if you're holding back on anything you have to give, stop. Worried about being judged for your oddball ideas? Skip it. In the end, you'll die anyway, and although people might miss you, nobody will really care about your insecurity, embarrassment, or uncertainty.

Your life will end, so if you have even the remotest idea about who you are and what you want to do, then be that and do that.

Sure, you always knew that. But I'm inviting you to know it in the deepest places inside you. Know it every moment. Dig into your spirit, dig into your gut, and get it.

* * *

Trust Your Gut

The first test of my new sense of knowing came quickly.

As soon as I healed, a surgeon who was tops in his field informed me that my clot had been caused by a structural abnormality in my left side, which didn't give my vein enough room for easy blood flow. He wanted to perform a surgery in which he would remove two of my ribs, to give my vein more room. He told me if I didn't have the surgery, I'd never be the "same" again. Without the surgery, I would have to restrict my activities and, even then, I would remain vulnerable to blood clots for the rest of my life.

I was scared. I felt vulnerable. It had been just over a week since I'd almost died, and here was an expert giving me advice on how I could prevent it happening again. Feeling pressured, and not ready to die, I agreed to have the surgery the next morning.

Then I walked out to a park bench, sat down, and became very still, not just outside, but also inside. I grew quieter than my own fear, until I felt myself fill with peace, not vastly different from the feeling I'd had when I left my body. And in that peaceful moment, I felt a clear answer rise from my gut. If it had been a physical voice, I like to think it would have boomed like James Earl Jones: "You don't need to get the surgery. You will be fine without it."

I trusted that voice. I now felt certain I didn't need surgery. What I needed was to change my lifestyle. It wasn't my body that had set me on a collision course with that blood clot, it was my unbalanced lifestyle. The doctor was an expert on the body, but I was an expert on me. And for the first time, I trusted that.

I marched back to the 10th floor of the hospital. In fact, I took the stairs, walked into the specialist's office unannounced, and blurted, "Sir, while I appreciate your advice, I'm choosing to not go through with the surgery."

He was irate.

He reminded me of the looming doom in my life if I didn't have the surgery. The madder he got, the more certain I felt about my choice. I understood he might be concerned at the possibility of my demise, but why was he so outraged over a decision that was mine to make?

In the face of the surgeon's expertise, some might have called my choice a serious case of denial. I knew that wasn't it. The way I knew was that my decision wasn't based in fear. I'd already died, and I wasn't afraid of that anymore. I wasn't avoiding surgery. In fact, I was certain I'd developed the clot because I'd been avoiding something more serious: my true path. I'd become unhealthy by denying my true self. I looked great on the outside, but my insides were churning. When I was miserable at work, I put on a phony gung-ho attitude. At the end of a hard day, when my instincts told me to go home and relax with a book, instead I went out for beers with clients. When I went to bed, I didn't get real rest, but woke in the middle of the night in a cold sweat.

Your body will rebel when you deny your true self. How could it possibly help my health to again ignore myself—the self who was screaming at me to change my life, and not expect some doctor to do it for me by cutting a chunk of me away. My decision was based on a gut-level recognition of what was true for me. I walked away from that angry doctor, and never looked back.

I haven't had a major health problem since. No clots. Nothing. I'm one of the healthiest, most active, most adventurous 51-year-old men I know. I take yoga, raft class five whitewater, run endurance races, traverse gorges, sky dive, ski big bumps, snowshoe, and hike the tallest peaks in the Rocky Mountains. At 49, I led the Aconcagua Man Project, a team of seven men who went on an expedition to Argentina to climb the nearly 23,000-foot Aconcagua, tallest mountain in the Andes.

Most of those feats wouldn't have been possible if I had said no to my truth and yes to another person's advice.

I'm not saying Western medicine is wrong. I still think it's important to seek advice from experts, including physicians. But ultimately our decisions belong to us. Ultimately we each have to take responsibility for our own lives. I've seen people who've had the surgery that I declined; to me it was as if someone took bricks away from the bottom of a house. The surgery probably helped some of them. But I needed to find balance within. I have no doubt I made the right decision.

Have you ever felt the pressure of a decision that could radically change your life? What decision are you facing now?

When I have a decision like that the first thing I do is my due diligence. That is, I gather as much information as I need to help me make an informed decision, from experts and informed sources. Often I discover equally compelling reasons for all of the choices before me. When that happens, there's only one source left to consider: me.

We all have the powerful ability to attune ourselves to our gut, to listen to that still, quiet voice inside that resonates with knowing. The truth this voice speaks may not be true for anyone but you. Experts may "tell" you your voice is absurd. But don't be swayed by people who call you crazy for daring to refer to yourself as a source of information in making choices.

Why not you?

You're the one who knows the history of your choices so far, and you're the one who has to live with the consequences of your next choice.

Make no mistake: this requires courage. It takes guts to follow your gut. But if I can do it, and if my clients can do it, then you can do it.

Get Real

Being attuned to self is not reserved for gurus. It's available to anyone willing to give up avoidance and listen inside for truth. You're the expert on your life. So, when you have a decision to make, once you've gathered the best info you can, trust your gut.

Here are two important keys to "gut listening":

1) Trust yourself more than you trust other people. This is not to say you should ignore counsel from others. It just means you get the final say. You are the one who determines your own actions.

2) Practice becoming grounded and quiet, so you can hear your gut talking. Sit long enough to ruminate on what feels both logical and intuitive. That is wisdom. When heart and head come together, it's because we are listening to the heart of God.

As with any skill, you'll get better at following your gut with practice. You'll get better at hearing your gut the more you listen. There are many ways to do this, including meditation, prayer, journaling, and simply sitting. Do whatever feels right for you.

If you're not sure which direction to go, I'm happy to offer one simple exercise to get you started. Think of a decision you need to make. Once you've done that, put down this book, go to a new location and sit. Then go through your body. Feel where your feet contact the floor, and then move up from there. As you move to each body part, notice how it's feeling. Don't try to make it feel differently. If it happens to relax on its own, just notice that, too. When you get to your head, notice your thoughts. Watch them float by. When you're ready, stop looking at your thoughts for a moment. If you can't, that's OK, just keep watching the thoughts float by until you're ready. As soon as you realize that you've stopped thinking for a moment, take a deep breath, and exhale—do this at least three times. Now, ask yourself which choice you want to make. If you're ready, go with that. If not, then come back tomorrow and give this process another go.

11

Get Real...
Get Physical

The Physicality of Leadership

Among the most important assets you possess as a leader are your strength and health.

If you've ever experienced serious illness, then you know what I mean.

I feel fortunate that there have been times in my life when I've experienced health problems. If you read that to mean that I see my experience of poor health as a good thing, you're correct. I don't think I'd appreciate my wellness nearly as much, if it weren't for the times when I needed to heal myself. I now pay close attention to my health, fitness, and well-being every day. I don't take my body for granted for a moment, because I know how crucial it is to my life's purpose and passion.

The brain that comes up with my ideas, the hands that write them down, the voice that communicates them, the legs that carry me to appointments, and, most important, the energy that moves me through each day, are all contained within my physical body. You might say that, at the most basic level, my body is the home in which I live, the primary office in which I get work done, and yes, the temple in which I connect with God.

My body is where my whole life begins and where all my experience comes to rest. If it's not in top working condition, I can't do the things I want to do to manifest extraordinary results.

If you ask a wise elder what he or she thinks is most important in life, you'll likely hear "your health" as one of the most common responses. Why? Because the elderly can look back and see that whenever their health fell apart, everything else was diminished.

Like any other worthy goal, long-term good health requires planning, focus, and effort to accomplish. Just as with any other goal, you cannot simply dream it into being.

This is about effort.

If you expect to make the effort to lead in extraordinary ways, then you also must make the effort to get physical. You must make the effort to schedule exercise. You can't let minutiae take over your day. You can't just keep saying you don't have time. You have to get up off your butt and make an effort to just do it, instead of sitting on the couch and deciding you're too tired.

If you can't lead yourself—if you can't lead your own body, then how can you lead others in all integrity?

The great Virgin Airlines leader and billionaire entrepreneur Richard Branson was taking questions at a gathering of young people eager to learn the secrets of his massive success.

One student asked him, "What is the surest way you know of to become more productive?" Branson's answer startled the group. He said, "Work out more."

Nutrition is also vital to great leadership. You have to find out what kinds of foods you like that are healthy, instead of assuming you can keep stuffing anything you want into your mouth. You have to put in the time it takes to buy and prepare healthy foods, instead of letting complacency take over in the form of junk foods, fast foods, and processed foods.

Effort leads in the direction of energy and life. Complacency leads in the direction of lethargy and morbidity.

I've seen people who spend so much time on the work, work, work of leadership that they ignore every other aspect—working excessive hours until exhausted, skipping lunch or grabbing a fast food burger, missing sleep due to worries over work, hitting the computer when what's needed is a walk or workout, staying indoors on weekends instead of hitting the trail or the courts. Some of these people become obese, others tired and out of shape, others just plain stressed out. Yet others develop stress-related illnesses, from flu to cancer.

It's a false worry that the time you invest in staying fit is time you could better spend on other goals. The truth is this investment will give you exponential returns in all areas of your life.

Some of us take our physical fitness for granted, and then feel blindsided when our bodies fall apart. But when we look back, we can see how our steps led us here.

Do yourself a favor and look forward now, instead of waiting to look back, and see where your current steps are leading. If it's the wrong direction, take another path. If you're a visionary leader intent on making a long-term difference, you owe it to yourself to prime your body for fitness. Physical fitness will imbue your entire physical self, body and mind, with the enthusiasm and stamina you'll need to complete your greatest projects and absorb life's most valuable lessons.

There's nothing shallow in caring about whether you look good and feel great. We're physical beings as much as we're mental and spiritual beings. All three work together to give our lives balance and lend our work meaning. Treat your body with respect, and it will work for you.

If you want the best results, both in your body and in your life, then go a step farther: push your body and test its limits—within a good trainer's guidance, of course. Through pushing your body to see what it can do, you'll develop both the physical and mental toughness to get yourself moving every day.

Make no mistake that mental toughness is part of the physical fitness equation. If you've ever run a footrace or climbed a mountain, you know what I mean. If you haven't, try it and you'll discover something amazing. It's not just your body's ability that factors into physical accomplishment, it's the mind's willingness to talk the body into continuing even after effort stops making sense, even after the goal of reaching the finish line begins to lose allure.

When we push our bodies beyond what we thought they could do, we train our minds to understand that we can also push ourselves to attain other goals beyond what we thought possible. In the mind-body-spirit continuum, the body can often lead the way.

And when you leave the body out of that triad, the other two elements suffer grievously.

Physical achievement produces character development. When we attain physical goals, we learn the kind of persistence and determination that will lead to achievement in all aspects of our lives.

Get Real

What is your health worth? What are you willing to do to stay healthy, or, if necessary, to heal yourself? Here's your challenge for this month:

If you don't exercise, add one day of exercise a week. Don't just say you'll do it; write it into your calendar or to-do list. Pick a specific day, time, and activity. If you typically hate exercise, then simply pick something fun that requires physical effort, like throwing a Frisbee with a friend, your significant other, or your kid. If you need a non-exercise incentive: try riding your bike to a place you want to go, like the movies. After you successfully make it through this month, up your exercise to two days a week next month.

If you already exercise regularly, but know you can do more, then add another day of exercise a week, or add another half-hour of exercise a day to your schedule. Don't just consider it part of your routine; include it on your calendar.

Make it just as important a part of your schedule as your client appointments and work deadlines.

Every time you think, "This is too hard," remember that's the point: this is a test of character, your chance to prove to yourself that you have what it takes to overcome any challenge. After you've discovered the energy, joy, and enthusiasm that come from feeling and looking better, remember that if you want those qualities to be a permanent part of your life, you must make your new fitness habits permanent. I invite you to come back to this chapter again and again to remind yourself of that, and to read this one line:

You can do it, and the only way to prove that to yourself is by, in fact, doing it.

12

Slowing Down To Speed Up

Get Distance to Gain Perspective

Sometimes when I face a major challenge, everything in my life becomes unclear. I feel like I'm driving on a mountain in the middle of a fog.

I'm talking about the kind of fog that's so thick you can't see anything more than a foot or two in front of you. You run the risk of going off the cliff, and all your panicked solutions, such as turning on the high beams or running the windshield wipers, only seem to make it worse.

Do you ever feel that way? Don't assume it means there's something wrong with your approach to life. Most of us feel that way from time to time.

But take comfort from me, someone who's been up that road many times and found the trick to not only surviving, but also thriving. I have learned to find, at the end of that foggy road, a place of new possibilities.

So, to me, the question isn't whether I'll ever feel lost. The question is: When I *am* lost, what will I do to regain my perspective so I can find my way?

Whenever I'm in a fog, I find that the greatest way to gain clarity is to *get some altitude.* What I'm saying is, I need to get higher than the problem, to rise above it and look down at it from a different point of view.

For years, I've been creating Culture Change Initiatives for companies. Those initiatives work. That's because the first thing I ask a team to do is to dig beneath their initial tensions and clarify what's going on under the surface.

For leaders, staying out of the fog of emotion can be powerful. I'm not suggesting leaders should be robots. I'm saying that many people get entangled in the emotional reactions to feeling trapped in a problem. Soon they become the very problem they want to solve. It's hard to solve an issue when you are the issue, so enmeshed with the problem at hand that you can't see it objectively anymore.

When you find yourself stuck in an ongoing problem, I recommend that you get away from the issue long enough to see it from a perspective that's more detached and realistic, rather than attached and emotional. Seek a higher consciousness.

When you step far enough away from the problem so that the fog is no longer clinging to you, you can create a bridge from which to observe. Standing on that bridge, you can stare at the rapids below and rely on your senses and reasoning to show you what those rapids are really made of: the dips, turns, rocks, waves, and eddies. From up high, you can map out the flow of things, decide what you need to do to navigate, and determine what kind of equipment and assistance may be of help, before you jump back into the whitewater and take on the situation.

This is the essence of getting real.

When you do return from your higher vantage point, you'll be able to handle yourself with calm assurance, because you've realistically assessed the conditions and made a plan.

I recently found myself in an email thread in which someone raised a work-related problem. In response, colleagues immediately "dug in" to positions, until everyone had built quite a trench to defend his position.

I was tempted to take a position myself! Instead, I detached and observed. The further I pulled out of the exchange, the funnier it seemed to me. I could see where people were dedicating themselves to being right, and spending hours stacking up arguments to prove it. What a waste of time!

I'm not saying I've never taken up a position based on the premise that I was right and all opponents were wrong. I can be adept at crafting an ironclad argument impervious to most debate. I can remember the self-righteous feeling in my gut when I would hit the send button—"I really nailed them this time!" Then, I'd wait eagerly for a response, to see what "they" would say back.

Would they be forced to see my unassailable logic? Would they dare try another fruitless argument? Would I find myself locked in a war of words with an equally stubborn opponent?

When I got into that frame of mind, and acted on it, the email exchange would often escalate into a bigger argument and hurt feelings. At the very least, my stomach would end up in knots, and theirs probably would, too. What a colossal waste of energy!

Wouldn't that energy be better spent on solutions and bridge-building? Instead, I was pointing my finger at unsolvable problems and trying to identify who screwed up what.

You might be thinking, "Sometimes it's not just that I need to be right—sometimes they *are* wrong!"

Maybe, maybe not. But when you're both that sure, how long do you want to keep pulling on your end of the rope, with no results?

Here's what I recommend: let the problem sit. I'm not saying to avoid it altogether. Just let it sit long enough for you to lose your attachment to the outcome, long enough to gain objectivity.

And remember: If the issue is big, *don't email*. Email is a venue that invites overstating, misinterpretation, and hubris. Instead, pick up the phone and call. A telephone requires us to use our manners and allows for nuanced communication.

My experience has been that usually you'll find a mutual solution within five to 10 minutes of good conversation. Isn't that better than spending a day or more spreading negative energy in dribs and drabs that suck the life out of you and your colleagues?

I recently faced a problem so big that I needed to get substantial distance from it in both space and time. For several days, I left my business behind for a trip deep into nature. My brothers and my friend Steve joined me. We backpacked 30 miles into Rocky Mountain National Park.

Surrounding myself with trees many generations old, massive rock that rose from the earth's crust long before human history, water that's part of the earth's endless lifecycle, and so many animals and plants that know nothing of my cares, I was able to tear down the walls within to reconnect with God.

The earth is both ancient and new, and when we open ourselves to its wonders, stripped of society's trappings, we gain both perspective and renewal. Everything seems fresh, clear, and bright.

After that trip, I saw everything in a new way, including the "problems" I'd left behind. When I returned, solutions flowed naturally from me as if they'd been there all along, and had only been trapped within me because I'd felt so trapped in the problem. The other people involved didn't see things exactly as I did, but my solutions didn't require them to. I did my part; the rest was up to them. The problem shrank, and I developed new options in my approach to dealing with people that will serve me in future.

Only when you completely set a problem aside for a while can you come back to that bridge with truly clarified vision. The only way to see better, is to stop looking for a while.

Take a moment and consider what issues in your life might benefit from a higher perspective. Do you need some time to walk away? A good night's sleep or a weekend with a good book? A few days in the mountains or at the beach? What can you do to give yourself the distance you need to see your problem decrease to a manageable size?

Do it.

When you return you may be surprised at how easy it is to map your way through the obstacles that seemed insurmountable an hour, a day, or a week before.

The Balanced Leader

There's a place deep inside of you that always knows the truth, or at least, my truth.

When I notice I'm moving too fast, that's usually an indication I'm trying to distract myself from something. That's my cue to slow down. It's time to tune in to what's going on internally.

Usually the thing I'm avoiding is the very thing I need to face. And if I don't handle it, I won't be able to move forward.

Slowing down can feel counterintuitive, especially when you're moving toward major goals. But that's when it's most important.

When you make the choice to slow down, you now have the time and space to look around you and ask questions. You can discover the issues you've been neglecting or avoiding. That's when your inner leader can emerge with clarity and resolve.

What are you trying to find? It may be different each time. But there's one thing I usually discover when I've been moving at high speed and finally stop to look around: I realize my life has gotten out of balance. Usually I've been giving too much attention to one part of my life and not the others. If I'm all work and no play, my work suffers. If I'm all play and no work, yes, my play actually suffers. If I neglect my relationships, my time alone is unproductive. If I neglect my alone time, my time with others lacks clear communication.

Frequently, I find that the slowing down in-and-of itself is what I needed. When I go too fast, I often rush past the lessons, solutions, and opportunities that are right in front of me. In short, I miss my whole life. What's the point to succeeding at an objective, if I miss my life? Isn't a fulfilling life the ultimate objective behind all the others?

Slowing down doesn't come naturally to me, as it doesn't to many Americans. For us, balanced living requires almost counterintuitive leadership. Sometimes a balanced lifestyle can feel downright lazy. It's easy to feel guilty, if we don't remind ourselves that down time is in service to productivity.

This is a lesson many of us may have to relearn for the rest of our lives. Have you noticed? Almost everything in our society points us toward doing everything faster. It's as if it's not even our choice anymore, as if we're on a conveyor belt, being carried toward more efficient living, whether we like it or not.

Do you often find yourself trying to keep up with "the list"? The list you created, or the one others created for you, the list you've written down or the one in your head, today's to-do list or the bucket list. I'm betting you have at least one. A list. I promise, if you're living to finish a list, you're not living in balance. Goals, plans, and lists are great, but if we're not careful they can become the distractions.

Meanwhile, the playtime, sleep, and lazy days we consider distractions can be critical steps toward our goals. If nothing else, those moments remind us of the joy of living that makes our goals worthwhile.

I recently visited a beautiful mountain resort. The leaves were golden, and there was a crisp hint of fall in the air. By spending just a few days surrounding myself with natural beauty, forcing myself to set aside all my lists and moving through my days without struggle, I found the place inside me that's balanced, rested, and calm.

When I ground myself in that place, I become simultaneously stronger in my business. I can serve people better from a place of inner strength and peace.

I once had the opportunity to ask a dying friend a provocative question. I asked, "As you look back on your life, what one thing would you have done differently?"

She said, "I would have said 'no' more to things I thought I had to say 'yes' to."

I never forgot the look in her eyes. It told me that I had a chance not to find myself feeling the same way on my deathbed. I took it, and ran with it, and that's my ongoing gift to her.

When I feel the imperative to slow down, I remember my friend's words, and say "no" more often. "No, I won't do that...No, I'm not available..."

We're not robots. We're human beings, who are, by the way, capable of many acts of creation that robots cannot duplicate. For humans, balanced living isn't a luxury; it's a necessity.

If we press ahead without making time for food and rest, laughter and love...if we don't take a break from creating and serving, so that we can enjoy the creations and services of others, we risk becoming overworked lunatics flailing in a sea of confusion.

You get to make a choice about everything that comes into your inbox.

Allow me to add a question to that box: How balanced do you feel right now? Don't be afraid to admit to yourself that your life feels out of balance. That's not a sin. It's just your mind, body, and spirit giving you a message: "Something needs adjusting."

It's in your power to adjust it. Seeing that you have the power to create balance is an effective form of getting real.

You have a choice to shape your own identity. Don't let yourself get pushed around by some image you're trying to live up to. Remember, in the end, you're in charge of your choices, because you're the one who has to live with the results—not your boss, mother, spouse, or even the IRS. It's not other people who take away our equanimity; only we can do that to ourselves, by allowing our lives to tip off balance.

I'll share a secret about leadership: I find that if I move on rebalancing my life sooner rather than later, it's a lot easier to move back to that soft spot of peace quickly. As a leadership guide, I've had enough practice to become very efficient at it.

What can you do to experience more peace and harmony in your life? Don't spend too much time pondering the question. Go with your gut. Whatever the answer is, do it. Not only will you be happier, you'll also lead other people more effectively.

Being There

Have you ever heard a song so moving that it sent a chill up your spine? Seen a sunset that brought tears to your eyes? Watched a movie so amazing that you texted your best friend before you left the theatre?

I'm blessed to have many such "inspired moments" in my life. They happen more often as I live more closely to my sense of Self, and as I slow down to appreciate them. But here's a potentially life-changing question:

Do those moments just happen or do we create them?

I'm convinced we create them.

I recently attended a course on coaching prosperity. The entire course was fantastic, but the second weekend was a 48-hour inspired moment. My veins were pumping nothing but goodness over the entire weekend. I don't believe those two days felt inspiring just because it happened to be a good class, but because the people in the class created it to feel miraculous. There were 12 of us who came together, and every single person *showed up.*

By "showing up" I don't mean that we all got on planes, flew to Phoenix, and attended the course. What I mean is, we all showed up completely, body, mind, and soul. Every single student brought complete generosity of Spirit to the table. I'll never forget the power of that weekend.

What made it so special?

There's something powerful about a group coming together with a common intention, and putting their full commitment behind it. Everyone in that room was intent on discovering what it would take to make a difference in the world, and then committing himself to doing it.

And I don't mean a small corner of the world, or a minor ripple of difference. What I'm talking about is true and expansive service to the world. That alone would have made it inspiring, but wait…there's more:

These were the type of leaders who don't apologize for who they are. They own their sense of self and share their convictions without concern for what others think. So, they not only shared their passion for service, but they did it from a place of "ownership" and personal responsibility, as opposed to establishing their positions by making other people feel inferior.

I heard freedom ringing throughout the room. These people were committed to dreams so vaulted they made my heart palpitate. By the time we were done, I had no doubt we could accomplish what we had set forth to do.

I hope you, too, will experience such an inspired moment. By buying this book, you've shown that you are ready for that kind of commitment at some level. Your moment may or may not come at a leadership conference, so I suggest you consistently stay in touch with your true self, your deepest passion, and your desire to be of service. That way, whenever a moment comes when you have no place to go but here, no place to be but now, and you can feel nothing but potential, you'll recognize it for what it is.

How will you know you're having an inspired moment? Here's a clue: it's the kind of moment that doesn't seem to move at all, while at the same time our insides feel alive with creative possibility, the sensation of connection with everything, and the ability to do anything. Although we know the inspired moment will ultimately call us to action, in the moment it's happening it only sits perfectly still and calls for nothing but aware breathing, peaceful surrender, and creative thought.

These moments are always available to us, if we're ready for them. Leaders create them consciously, whenever the moment feels right. It's important to grow still and let the inspiration sink in.

When we don't give ourselves those moments, we tend to get too serious. Nothing is funny anymore. Everything is a hassle. So if you want to create and lead awe-inspiring action, first give in to the quiet stillness of the inspired moment.

Get Real

When it comes to inspired moments, anytime can be the right time. Are you ready? Then stop right now and create one. Start by simply appreciating yourself, where you are in this moment, both in your life and in your physical surroundings. Then get out of your head, sit still for two full minutes, and do nothing. Just *be* there. When you're done with your moment of stillness, apply yourself to the next right thing you need to do today. It's possible your idea about what that is may have changed between the time you started this exercise and the time you finished it. If so, great. The inspiration is working.

If not, don't worry. There will be other opportunities. You can always do the above exercise again. Sometimes we have to go through the motions of an activity several times, before we find the key that makes it work for us. Don't force it. Just keep coming back to "being there." When you're ready, it will give something to you.

If you'd like to get a better handle on what I mean by "being there," allow me to suggest you rent the movie, *Being There*. If you haven't seen it, allow me to warn you, the first time I saw it I hated it. It moved too slowly for me. I wanted action. I wanted someone to entertain me. But I still sensed something profound there, so I watched it again. The second time, I slowed down, slowed my thoughts and expectations, so I could *be there* with the movie. Once I did that, I no longer needed to be entertained. I was just there. Watch the movie, and keep the title in mind. Remember this is about being. When you can hang with it, go back to the inspired moment exercise and do it again.

Then be ready for all the inspired moments, whenever and wherever they come.

13

Some Small Stuff Deserves a Little Sweat

How Do You Like Your Coffee?

One day I walked into a coffee shop that touts the piping hot freshness of its fine coffees, and bought myself a cup.

It was lukewarm. Bordering on cold.

There was a time in my life when I would have let that slide. What's more, I would have prided myself on choosing peace over principle.

The problem is that appeasing people rarely leads to true peace. If I'd walked away with cold coffee from that company that promised the hot stuff, it wouldn't have been about maintaining peace, but about avoiding discomfort...being too lazy to speak up.

But laziness doesn't serve anyone.

So I told the barista that my coffee was cold, and asked for a new one. She apologized and replaced it.

This was an opportunity for that employee to discover any number of things: from something as simple as malfunctioning equipment, to the importance of quality and customer service.

If a business doesn't ensure that its company culture is instilling the values of quality and service, from top management down to the person at the counter, then that business is on a path to failure.

As the founder of Microsoft, Bill Gates, has said, "Your most unhappy customers are your greatest source of learning."

When customers draw mistakes to a company's attention, that company has an opportunity to reevaluate its performance and its values.

When, as customers, we say nothing, we rob the company of an opportunity to make an improvement, and we lose an opportunity to reaffirm our own commitment to the truth.

Why should I pay something for nothing? What does that say about how I value myself and others? What effect does that have on my self-esteem?

It's tempting to say that one cup of coffee isn't worth bothering with. It's just one detail, right? But the whole picture of life is made up of details!

Coffee might be just one beverage in my day, but it's also one beverage in the day of millions of people, 365 days a year, and it represents a multi-billion dollar industry. That business involves coffee growers, pickers, buyers, sellers, distributors, corporate heads, managers, advertisers, restaurants and coffee houses, waitresses and baristas, and coffee drinkers.

Is it the end of the world?

No. But if Dunkin' Donuts, Starbucks, or Caribou Coffee made a habit of serving lukewarm coffee like mine was, they would eventually lose their customers and their market positions, and a lot of people would lose jobs and investments.

So you see, plenty of people are invested in that one cup of coffee.

This is how it is for most businesses. If they miss the mark on quality or service once or twice, it might not be a big deal. But over time, it's exactly how reputations are built: one cup or one gallon, one widget or one car, one deal or one project at a time.

One prevailing aphorism of our time is "Don't sweat the small stuff." There's some wisdom in that approach. Because it's not worth ruining relationships over petty grievances, not worth waging war over a slight.

But when it comes to our desire to be of service in this world, the small stuff *is worth the sweat.*

In fact, at the leadership level I want to live, "Don't sweat the small stuff" is actually backwards. Everything that looks like small stuff adds up to big stuff—say, your life or your business.

When we avoid sweating the small stuff, we often avoid the transformation that we might achieve, or help others achieve, through dealing with an opportune situation.

Sweating the small stuff is the way we exhibit our commitment to something greater.

For example, a lot of leaders say, "We're committed to excellence." Yet, when a client complains, those same "leaders" make excuses, pass the buck, and even try to blame the customer.

Some people standing behind me in that coffee line, and even some baristas standing in front of me, might roll their eyes at my wasting time over something so inconsequential as tepid coffee:

"Is that little cup really worth the fuss?"

It is. Because if my coffee is tepid, it's going to be the same for everyone who hits the dispenser after me. This is how minor inconveniences turn into major problems.

And this is not about anger or emotion. I didn't have to freak out over the cold coffee. I didn't shout or make a scene. As a customer, I just pointed out that it wasn't hot, and that I wanted a fresh cup.

If I had been a manager in that coffee joint, I might have used the chilly coffee as a teaching point about quality. If I were a corporate leader who witnessed that sort of moment, I might suggest the entire company revisit quality control.

Starbucks is America's prevailing coffee chain giant. Yet in the final quarter of 2007, Starbucks' sales growth slowed to an all-time low. When that happened, Starbucks returned to its roots: quality. On the night of February 26, 2008, the coffee giant closed 7,100 stores for three hours to retrain some 135,000 employees, primarily baristas.

What did the managers teach them?

New standards to create the perfect espresso shot, steam the milk, and get every element in every cup just right. We're talking about such details as making sure it takes 15 to 19 seconds for each shot to pour from the machine so it comes out like honey dripping from a spoon, to never let shots sit for more than 10 seconds, and to never re-steam milk. Managers also reminded baristas of some basics of customer service, like smiling and saying thank you. Talk about sweating the small stuff.

By the second quarter of 2011, Starbucks was reporting renewed record revenue growth.

Expressing displeasure or disappointment need not require being rude or creating conflict. There's no need to browbeat a customer service professional because your baggage is lost. That person didn't set out on a campaign to hurt you. By the same token, there's no need to shout at, blame, or threaten employees when sales are flagging. It's enough to simply speak the truth about what isn't working, and then create a new plan for what might make things work.

I remember receiving an email from a blog subscriber who had become a friend. He wrote me an email sharing his point of view on one of my posts. He liked some things I'd said, but not others. His email gave me food for thought, and I realized that there were some points on which I could have been clearer. Because he took the trouble to communicate his truth with me, I had a chance to reflect and communicate back, and from that response we gained a better understanding of each other. This is a powerful way to respond to complaints.

I realize not everyone will react that way to the truth. But I encourage you not to let that frighten you away from speaking your truth, even about the small stuff. You'll likely find that those who are responsive are the kind of people who have the most to offer in any relationship, business or otherwise.

No, not everyone is willing or ready to deal with the honest give-and-take of information that can contribute to creating better businesses, better relationships, and a better world. But wouldn't you rather be part of the circle that is?

How to Fix a Broken Wheel

Sometimes telling the truth is just the beginning.

Sometimes when we know the truth about what needs to be done, we are also the ones who have to get off our butts and do something about it.

One day I was driving home and singing along to one of my favorite songs on the radio, feeling peaceful as I contemplated a relaxing evening.

Then, as the garage door opened, I stopped singing.

Something dreadful loomed in front of me.

It had been sitting there for months, judging me, gloating at my inadequacy and my laziness. I'd seen it maybe a hundred times before, and I knew what needed to be done.

Yet I'd done nothing.

It was a lawnmower with a broken wheel.

The day I'd first discovered that broken wheel, I'd told myself, "I need to fix that wheel."

Then I thought, "I'll fix it later."

That was more than six months earlier, and now my nemesis had become so powerful it had silenced my song and darkened my mood.

I had turned my lawnmower into an *incomplete* in my life, and incompletes rob me of creative energy.

How many incompletes do you have in your life?

I'm talking about things you know you need to handle, yet resist handling.

Sometimes we'll deal with the gnawing discomfort of procrastination for months, rather than deal with 10 minutes of "have to." But make no mistake, when you put things off that you believe must be done, it steals the joy and creativity from other parts of your life. Why? Because your better Self keeps track of your internal promises.

I knew I hadn't fixed that broken wheel, and every time I saw it became a subtle reminder of a broken promise to myself.

Here's the terrible truth about things we don't want to do that have to be done: if we're waiting until we feel like it, we'll never do it.

I most likely will never wake up and say, "Today, I feel like fixing the wheel on that old lawnmower."

Meanwhile, when you're waiting to feel like taking care of that one irritating item, a slew of others will follow on its heels, until the weight of all you've left undone threatens to make you feel so overwhelmed you don't want to do anything at all.

When we resist completion long enough it leads to numbness, inertia, freezing up.

Let's get real about the simplest yet hardest thing that leaders do.

Leaders complete things.

Leaders do what they say they're going to do.

Since I left that lawnmower sitting there for six months, does that mean I'm not a leader? No. The fact that I care enough that it bugged me until I dealt with it shows that I know I'm a leader, and I'm not willing to settle for less than completion.

I finally told myself that lawnmower would not fix itself, so I had one of five choices: 1) Decide I don't give a hoot about the broken wheel, 2) Buy a new lawnmower, 3) Pay someone to fix it, 4) Figure out how to fix it myself, or 5) Do nothing and continue to feel frustrated every time I walk into the garage.

I chose option four and fixed it myself.

I am not suggesting you should fix all the broken wheels in your life, unless you want to. When taking action, that's an important thing to consider: do you want to? Once you know that, it's easier to complete the task.

When you ask yourself that question, remember to consider the consequences if your option is not number four: How will you feel if you do nothing? Are you willing to live with that?

Whatever you do, do yourself a favor, don't wait until you feel like it to deal with the stuff that you believe needs doing.

And let's get real about the time element. How long does it really take to fix a broken wheel, or to handle most of the incompletes in your life?

In most cases, not long!

I spent many more frustrating moments (not) fixing that stupid wheel in my head than it took to fix it in reality—all of 10 minutes.

What incompletes are you avoiding?

Here's some motivation to help you pick one and move on it: **Incompleteness creates chaos, but completion releases energy and creates freedom.**

I've experienced this for myself, and I've seen it in my clients: completion builds momentum, and gets us in touch with our priorities, which are usually much more important than lawnmowers—even more important than, say, a hot cup of coffee.

Get Real

For the next week, I invite you to stop appeasing others. The next time you have an opportunity to tell someone something that will help you get what you want while giving them an opportunity to be of better service, make the choice to speak up. Before you speak up, make sure you have three things firmly in mind: 1) You will not shout or lose your temper, 2) you will not blame but simply state the facts of what went wrong and what you would like to have happen to make it right, 3) you only wish to be of service to yourself and the other person/people involved. Now, go out there and say it like it is.

In the meantime, I suggest that you deal in a little truth telling with yourself. What is one item you know you need to take care of to move forward in life, but which you've been avoiding. Make it the next item on your to-do list for today. Don't allow others to distract you. Practice your power of focus. Be sure you work on that broken wheel until it's fixed.

You don't need to think ahead to the whole list, as that's just another form of self-torture. Just do that one thing, and do it now.

After you do that, I invite you to try one of my favorite traditions, which I call "Completion Day." It's pretty simple. Grab your calendar, pick a day, and label it "COMPLETION DAY." Then make a list of things you can complete during a five-hour period, conservatively. Some things may take longer than you thought, but most of the things you've been avoiding will probably take less time than you thought. At the end of the day, if you worked at least five hours and finished half the items on your list, reward yourself. Then make note of the rewards Completion Day keeps giving you in the days to come, as you gain creative energy from your new clean slate.

14

Never, Never, Never, Sometimes Quit

At Times, Quitting is for Champions

Something worth starting can often change into something not worth finishing.

I rarely quit something worth starting. But I have done it before, and I will again, without shame. Not because I'm a quitter, but because sometimes I find myself in the middle of something that no longer serves me or anyone else.

I'd wager that most people have quit something in their lives at some point. Sometimes they quit because they lack discipline or self-confidence, or because they fear responsibility or failure. But I've also witnessed many instances when people *fail* to quit even when they know they should. Often they fear someone will make those very judgments: that they lack discipline or confidence, that they're irresponsible or failures.

I've also seen people who have the courage to quit when they know it's the right thing to do: people who refuse to continue on a course of action when they receive new evidence that contradicts the information on which they based that course of action.

Sometimes a course of action may be a good one in theory, but this may not be the right timing, or certain people may not be right for the job.

Although I usually counsel people against arguing for their limitations, from time to time I do catch a few biting off more than they can chew.

Is there something in your life you should quit right now?

I'm not talking about obvious things like smoking or heavy drinking.

I'm talking about situations where you've banged your head so hard against the wall that you've bruised your spirit. That can be a good time to step back and stop doing what isn't working anyway. That can be a good time to get real.

Can you believe this? A leadership coach who is all about action suggesting that you quit?

That's right. Because quitting is an action, too.

It can be an action that frees you from pursuing things that are an energy drain and time drain. It can put you back on a path where you commit to more effective action.

One of the historic figures I admire is Winston Churchill. He was a wise leader who earned the deep respect of Britain and the world by showing the maturity of a statesman in times of crisis.

On the other hand, he once said, "Never, never, never, never give up," and I disagree.

It may have been an inspirational call to perseverance at the time, but it's a ludicrous saying to apply to every situation.

Surely you can think of a time in history when the best course of action would have been to quit.

Adhering blindly to the philosophy of "never give up" can lead to ineffective, misguided leadership. A great leader must be willing to evaluate each situation on its merits and consider all the alternatives, including the alternative of giving up.

Borders bookstores ran its company into the ground by not knowing when to quit. They blindly persevered with the hope that downloadable digital books and Amazon were a passing fancy, and sooner or later people would return to the hardcover and paperback books bought in their stores. A classic failure to get real.

Flexibility is more important than ever in modern leadership. Things are not as predictable today as they were 25 years ago. Technology has made it possible to exchange information, take action, and produce results faster, and on a wider scale, than ever before.

That means that wrongheaded "persistence" can lead to dire consequences very quickly. It soon becomes what Emerson called a "foolish consistency."

In our global economy, an existing business direction can change in moments. Having the strength and self-possession to know when to say "I quit" has never been more important.

Have you ever held on tightly to a decision because you feared others would accuse you of being a quitter? Have you ever kept going when you knew you should stop?

Sometimes quitting can put you in a thankless position. Others who fear change may turn their backs on you. Some who don't agree with you will fight you. Some people with selfish motives may try to damage your reputation to build their own.

But, if you have the courage of your conviction, quitting a wrong course is the only path for real leadership to take. Take comfort in this: When you act with conviction, you'll attract followers who appreciate your strength.

Most of the time staying the course reaps tremendous rewards.

But what if you're on a golf course all the time and you discover you hate golf?

If it were me, I'd stop trying to score a hole in one and instead get out my fly rod.

When we take an honest look at our lives, from time to time we find that we're in the middle of a game we don't enjoy. Not because we're dishonest, but because we let the influences around us drown out our inner voice.

It's great to surround yourself with a circle of trust: parents, bosses, friends, experts, social circles, political leaders, society. Yet even the best and brightest of those you trust can embrace ideas that are right for them but not for you. It's always up to you to consult your own internal compass.

It's saddest, I think, when we find that the pressure to stay a wrong course doesn't come from outside influences but from within: old memories and past hurts that make up an ego afraid to look like a quitter. We may perceive that we'll be letting someone down, when in actuality that worry is a reverberation of guilt over letting someone down in the past.

When you're facing a decision on whether or not to change course, it's another time when getting some distance can help. Get out of the emotion of the situation, step away from the people involved, and find a space alone to evaluate what's really going on.

You may find that you've been living with an illusion about what you're doing, based on an emotional need to see things in the best possible light. In that case, seeing the reality can be painful. But seeing things *as they are* is necessary to making an informed choice.

Don't let yourself be seduced by rationalizations like "it could be worse," or "this is the last time," or "we need the work." On that path, integrity eventually becomes soft as corn mush. If you want to exercise your integrity, consider this: do you love yourself and those around you enough to be honest about what feels right to you?

I've seen many people stay in a job they hated for years because they were afraid to quit.

Yes, quitting can be scary. In the recent recession, some people with solid resumes found themselves pounding pavement for two years. Yet when you do work you hate for people you don't respect, just because you're afraid of what will happen if you stop, it becomes a form of psychological slavery—a slavery of your own making.

Why do that to yourself?

So many Americans have sacrificed so much for freedom, it seems cowardly to let our fears stop us from doing what our Declaration of Independence claims it is our right to do: pursue happiness.

And, no, that declaration does not include a promise that you'll achieve happiness. But how can you achieve it if you don't pursue it? And how can you pursue it, if you're still cowering under the cover of some other pursuit that makes you miserable?

If you decide to quit, it's important to do it in a way that maintains your integrity—especially when you're engaged in an endeavor that is still an honorable course for the other parties involved. Remember two things: 1) Don't lie about why you're quitting, and 2) Do your best to negotiate quitting terms that serve all parties.

Quitting does not make you a loser.

When a champion athlete breaks an ankle, he or she quits the race in service to a higher value. The champ can't run on a broken ankle and expect to excel in the many races still ahead. That person is not a quitter. That athlete is still a champion, who simply needs to let an ankle heal before taking on another race.

One of my friends quit his marketing job to become a life coach. He loves it. He was not a leader as a marketing director, but he is a leader in the coaching community. In marketing, he'd become a slave to a choice he'd made years before, a choice that no longer fit. Let his experience illuminate this truth for you: **When you're honest about who you are and what you want, and pursue that with passion, that is freedom.**

When you have the courage to quit the wrong path, you serve all of us. When you quit something unhealthy to pursue a path that's enlivening, you become an inspiration to everyone who crosses your path. When you make a dash for freedom, you ring the Liberty Bell for us all.

As a leader, the most important person you'll ever lead is yourself. Answering to yourself requires rigorous internal listening, disengagement from unhealthy situations, and freeing yourself to embrace life more fully.

What's Your 20/80?

I recently found myself beating my head against the same wall of habit and not getting any results, just a bruised head.

Do you know what it feels like to spend 80 percent of your time on a 20 percent result? It doesn't feel very smart, does it?

It's not smart for me, because I value making a difference in my work and I've found that 80 percent of the results in my life come from 20 percent of my focus.

You may recognize that I'm piggybacking on Pareto's Principle, theorized by the great Italian economist Vilfredo Pareto. Pareto's research showed that 20 percent of our effort produces 80 percent of our results in life. While his work predominantly applied to projects, resources, time, and management, I see a deeper application.

The deeper application of Pareto's Principle has to do with the people in our lives. Have you noticed that spending time with some people leaves you feeling lifted and inspired, while spending time with others leaves you feeling drained?

Most of these other people are energy leeches, resistant to help or change. No matter how much joy you bring to the table, no matter how compassionate you are, no matter how much service you render, they continue to carry that dark cloud—and they continue to leech your energy.

They may seem pitiable, but deep down you sense the truth: most of them are selfish.

Energy leeches take more than they give. They waste most of a conversation talking about what's not working for them and why it will never work, instead of focusing on what is working and finding ways to turn the problems around so they work, too.

Sometimes they're right about the problems, but here's the catch: when you offer solutions, they shoot down every one, staying attached to the idea that nothing works.

So how does this relate to the 20/80 principle? These people reverse Pareto's equation. Energy leeches suck up 80 percent or more of the energy and enthusiasm that are so vital to you as a leader.

Some energy suckers have been so traumatized in early life that their negativity has become very hard to overcome. But that doesn't lessen their negative impact on you.

Consider this: if you see a panicked drowning victim and you jump in after them, it's a natural reflex for them to pull you down with them, drowning two people instead of one. Unless you're a trained expert, your best bet is to just throw them a life preserver and leave the rest to them.

An energy leech is like that drowning victim. The only trained expert who might be able to help is a therapist. Unless you're a therapist, there may be no effective way for you to help them. If you don't want to drown with them, stay out of the water.

You only get one shot at this precious life, so you need to make a choice: Are you going to let people drain most of the energy you have to offer, leaving you incapable of being much good to anyone? Or are you going to say, "I'm so sorry I can't help you!" and move on to those for whom you can truly be of service.

Cutting energy-draining people and situations out of your life can be done with loving detachment and grace, and without criticism. You can recognize that they truly are suffering, but that you can't help them.

In fact, your efforts to help may even be hindering them from getting better. By continuing to give in to their life-draining habits, you are only delaying their chance for real change.

We all want to help and to be liked, which makes it hard to walk away from people who seem to need so much. But if you look at your past relationships, you'll recall that such people have always taken an inordinate amount of your own physical, emotional, and mental energy. Yet in the end, they didn't feel much better. And you felt much worse!

That math doesn't add up.

So you can serve both parties by walking away.

And be aware that the leech may lash out, accusing you of selfishness. Don't be fooled. It's a false accusation and a trap. Just keep walking.

I recently found myself in the clutches of an energy leech. Usually I wake up eager to greet the day, but one morning I woke with a heavy heart. It wasn't anybody's fault, not even mine. I just became aware that I felt hopeless. I asked myself why, and realized it was because I was working with certain clients who claimed they were interested in growth, but who were only interested in convincing me of how unsolvable their problems were.

I concluded that I had to cut them loose.

The gist of what I told them was that we were not a right fit for each other. My commitment to their success exceeded their own. That was true.

I invite you to cut loose those relationships that are taking 80 percent of your energy for only 20 percent of your results. Start focusing on the places where you can leverage your energy more efficiently. When you can turn that number around, and put in 20 percent positive energy for an 80 percent positive outcome, we're talking some miraculous math. That means you'll still have 80 percent of your energy left, and if you use it wisely, you can get results that beat 100 percent.

I'm not talking about giving up on someone when the going gets tough. I'm talking about moving on after you've done all you can. And when it comes to energy leeches, the faster you move the better. Avoidance will only rob you of more time and energy. And it will rob them of the opportunity to maybe, just maybe, notice that their tactic isn't attracting the help they want.

Only they can change themselves.

All you can do is get out of the way.

This is your chance to clarify your priorities and consciously devote your time to efforts that enliven your spirit, and the spirit of your team.

Consider this: due to the 20/80 principle, you'll spend less energy while achieving more results. All you have to do is stop spending excess energy on people who are dedicated to their own misery, and switch to spending your energy on people who appreciate your time and who are committed to results. Do that, and you'll see your world turn upside down—in the best possible way.

Get Real

Get out a blank sheet of paper and get ready to answer a question and make two lists. Use one side of the paper for the question, and the other side for the lists. Here's the question: what's the most important thing you want to offer to the world? Don't get distracted by your heavy heart over your current situation or your inability to believe in a different future. Just describe what you would offer if you could.

Now divide the blank side of the page into two columns. At the top of the first column write the word "Invite," and at the top of the second column write the word "Quit." Under the word "Invite," list all the people and activities that you can focus on in your life right now that will take you closer to attaining the vision you described on the other side of the page. Then under the word "Quit," list all the people and activities in your life right now that will take time or energy *away* from your pursuit of that vision. Look at your first list: those are the people I suggest you commit your energy to in the course of the next year. Now look at your second list: those are the people and activities I suggest you find ways to cut loose from your life during the next year.

You have just chosen where you're going to spend at least 20 percent of your energy, and where you're going to get back at least 80 percent of your energy. When the year is up, come back to this chapter and try the exercise again. If it's easier next time, that's because it's working. Celebrate.

15

Endless Possibility

The Creativity of Leadership

"I can't do that"…"I don't have the right job"…"It's too hard."

As a Leadership Guide, I hear these kinds of excuses every day. None of them are true. Yet they often seem true, because the kind of thinking required to say them is the kind of thinking that stacks up evidence to prove that the thinker is "right."

But stacking up reasons why something can't be done never has as much power as saying, à la Han Solo, "Never tell me the odds." OK, *Star Wars* is a movie, but consider the real stories of these real people:

- Wilma Rudolph was told she would never walk, due to the crippling effects of polio. She became an Olympic runner who won three gold medals and was named "The Fastest Woman in the World."

- Louisa May Alcott was turned down by countless publishers, who told her that nobody would ever read her now-classic children's book, *Little Women*.

- President Abraham Lincoln began his service in the Blackhawk War as a captain, but by the end of the war he had been demoted to private. In fact, he suffered many setbacks on his way to becoming one of America's greatest leaders.

Thought creates its own trajectory, leading to words and actions that follow through on that heading. Thinking "it's not possible" or "it's not realistic" is like pointing your life toward a downturn.

I'm a compassionate man. I understand the humility, self-doubt, and real-life pressures that can lead someone to say of their dreams, "It can't be done." And while I do understand it, I just don't believe it.

If you have an idea, a vision, a dream, it would not come into your brain unless yours was a brain capable of taking the steps to lead you to it. Walt Disney famously said (and proved in his life): "If you can dream it, you can do it."

Real dreams come into your head because your head knows you can make them real. You just have to get out of the idea's way, and not let those other thoughts in your head kill it before it has a chance to fly.

Those other thoughts, the self-limiting ones, are there to protect you from things like wild animals, armed thugs, and hitting the beach without your sunscreen—not to protect you from your own dreams.

And you have to tell that protective part of your mind to be quiet when it's not needed, wanted, or useful.

That's why having a coach is so powerful. Sometimes we're too close to a situation to be able to tell the difference between the realistic thoughts that keep us grounded and the limiting ones that lead to fear or complacency.

A great coach will mirror back to you where you're limiting your Self.

That's why you'll rarely see me react with irritation when I hear clients talk negatively about their abilities and possibilities. There's a transparency to that kind of consciousness; it allows me to see through the fear to what their brain really wants to work on.

And I know that behind the expression of fear, on its flip side, is a glimpse of the immense power within.

Often a person who says, "I could never do that," is actually saying: "I'm afraid of what I might create if I really put my best Self forward."

Thinking and saying "I can't do it" asks nothing of you. It suggests no action at all. Therefore it keeps you safe in your comfort zone.

However, "What if I did do it?" can ask a lot of you. A dream suggests a next action. It asks you to account to yourself. When you speak it aloud it even asks you to account to others.

No wonder so many people say, "I can't."

But there's not much life to be lived in "I can't."

So, when people tell me, "I can't do that," that's when I hear the Leadership Bat Phone start to ring!

Sometimes my next step is to ask them to shift that sentence just slightly, and ask the question, "What if I *did* do it?" That question is the first step into a whole new way of looking at their vision—because whether they're saying "I can't" or "I can," they're still talking about their vision. And once you've had a vision of what *could happen* there's no forgetting it. So why try?

One day, one of my clients came to my office upset because he didn't have a job.

"I have to get a job," he said. "I have to go to work for somebody…find someone who will hire me and take me on."

"Why do you have to do that?" I replied. "Look around your world and see all the work that needs to be done. Go do that work yourself and charge a fee for it."

This is an inquiry that can change an employee into an entrepreneur. It can change a person who rides the ups and downs of an economy to someone who helps design the ride.

Let's look at an example of that idea:

During the recent economic downturn, Jean Spencer was working at a journalism internship in Washington D.C., and facing one of the coldest winters she'd ever experienced, even though she was from Colorado. She kept missing calls from her editor whenever she was outdoors or riding public transportation, because she was wearing gloves, and gloves don't work on touchscreen devices like her iPhone. By the time she would manage to bite off her gloves, shove them into her coat, and pull out her phone, the calls would have gone to voice mail.

She expressed her frustration to her mother, Jennifer Spencer, saying something to the effect of, "Someone needs to invent a glove that will work with a touchscreen."

Her mother was an entrepreneur and artist from Boulder. After pondering her daughter's expression of frustration, she started researching how to make a glove that would conduct the bioelectricity in a person's hand, which is what's required to make touchscreen technology work.

Eventually mother and daughter invented and designed the Aglove®, a silver and nylon glove that does the trick.

They found an investor who recognized that it was a perfect idea whose time had come.

Mother and daughter started selling gloves in September of 2010. By February of 2011 they'd sold some 60,000 pairs of gloves in 43 countries, and hired a staff of five. Many customers have told them that they'd been wondering when someone was going to come up with something like this. And they started it all during the toughest economic times since the Great Depression.

And you don't have to quit your company to enjoy the fruits of entrepreneurial thinking. If you already have a job that you love, you can still apply the same idea: Find a need or want, and fill it.

A person with good ideas is a person who can become a rock star at work. Even small ideas can stand out, because so many employees spend their workdays using their creativity to find ways to avoid work.

People who think and act creatively inspire creativity in others. Think of the shift that could occur in our collective awareness as leaders if we all changed our approach from "What has been done before," or "Why that idea won't work," to "What if we tried something new?" Consider the people around you who might be hiding their ideas from the light of day, for fear that someone might shoot them down.

If we could be the courageous example of someone who creates something from nothing, we would be even more inspiring as leaders. Creating new opportunities is more powerful than simply working on what's handed to you. When you show up with a desire and willingness to create, you'll notice that the hours don't crawl by at work anymore. When you switch from a position of "What is my assignment for today?" to "What possibilities can I create today?" the process becomes self-perpetuating. Creating new possibilities leads to more possibilities.

Don't wait for self-doubt to disappear. Doubts will always float around your brain. Ignore them. Or shout them down: "You can't get the best of me!"

And don't wait for perfect opportunities to fall into your lap. Lucky opportunities do show up sometimes, but luck is fickle, so don't count on it. Besides, when luck does come, it usually smiles most brightly on those who have been planning for it.

Gratitude: The Key To Freedom

Gratitude is a direct conduit to success. Without it you can't sustain forward motion in your life.

Notice that you work hard to reach your goals. You reach some, but not all of them. Because this world is so conditioned to look at what we *don't* have, you therefore focus on what's not working. And when you focus long enough on that negative viewpoint, your work life begins to feel meaningless.

My own work life is successful beyond anything I used to imagine, but I'm also human and susceptible to the same temptations as other people—including the temptation to obsess about all the things in my life that are *not* working.

So how do I get unstuck?

I've trained my mind to treat cynical thoughts the way a Teflon pan treats sticky proteins: it lets them slide in and out without sticking.

You may be thinking: *Sure that sounds great, but those negative thoughts just come up on their own, so how can I control them?*

Maybe you can't control which thoughts appear. But you can do something about how long they stick around.

Just notice when they do appear, and gently but deliberately follow them up with another thought.

Try this: Every time you're hit with a thought about how you've failed, what's missing, or why your dreams aren't possible, follow that thought with one of gratitude.

You'll begin to notice a shift in your mindset.

By shifting your mind, you make room for the ideas, goals, and plans that can lead you toward success.

What can you be grateful for?

Everything.

Not just successes, but failures, too. Not just everything you have, but everything that's missing.

The moment you find yourself mourning your past failures and losses, or fearing future failures and losses—you can acknowledge those thoughts, but then immediately follow them up with a thought of gratitude for anything in your life that you can think of at that moment.

I mean anything.

Anything you've experienced, learned, produced, seen, not seen, been, not been, done, not done. Be grateful for the gifts in your life and the achievements you've made. But also challenge yourself to honestly consider what kind of strength your losses and failures have given you.

You won't ever be able to get rid of all negative thoughts. Knowing that is one of the benefits of getting real! But what you can do is gain gratitude. Without gratitude, there's no way to rise above the obstacles in your life. Even if you run up a mountain halfway around the world, you'll just bring all your issues with you, and carry them around like a backpack full of rocks. I know; I've been there.

When I feel appreciation for the world I inhabit, the objectives I have obtained, and even all I have failed to achieve, I open myself to the blessings that prevail, as well as those blessings that are still out there waiting for me to grasp them.

Finding gratitude need not be another dreary task on your to-do list, either. You don't need to structure a list, or schedule prayer time, or learn to meditate (though that's a great idea), or do anything time-consuming. I'm simply suggesting that each time you find your brain chewing on negativity, throw a few bites of gratitude in there, and just chew for a few minutes until the bitter taste is gone. There's no need to wrack your brain. Simply and immediately recall your connection to the things in your life that have meant the most to you, for better or worse. Then notice the energy and enthusiasm building and restoring you to good balance.

Don't try to force this process. Just gently turn your mind and heart toward the things you love and let the energy flow naturally.

When I feel grateful and appreciative for my life, the feeling isn't like pushing against the current of negativity. Instead, it's like jumping into a river and letting myself float with the current, flowing with the stream.

Even if you don't see results right away, stay with the practice. I promise you will soon start to feel better and more satisfied with who you are and where your life is. And there's no way around it: people who feel relaxed and happy are more productive.

Gratitude is your key to freedom. Is that a spiritual idea? That's up to you. You can be grateful to God, to everyone, to yourself...or you can simply feel gratitude for its own sake.

I would suggest this: if it's spiritual to live by a principle with the power to shift your entire state of being, then gratitude is spiritual. Whenever I feel gratitude, my internal sense is that it does feed my spirit. However, my mind understands that it doesn't matter whether this practice is labeled as "spiritual" or not. What matters is that it produces results. Practicing gratitude works.

Get Real

The next time you find any area of your life in a slump, try this experiment in gratitude: take note of how your day's activities have been going so far. Now, stop and make a list of the five things you're most grateful for that day. Make it easy on yourself this time by picking only happy things as the objects of your gratitude, but any happy things you want: funny friends, generous family, a supportive boss or coworker, your morning run, a clever idea you had today, a great movie you rented for tonight, plans to hike this weekend, a sunny day, a delicious piece of chocolate. Once you've made your list, go back to your day's activities. Make note of how your day goes after that. Notice your mental acuity. Take note of your emotional state. Consider how productive you are.

If you find that your day improves, then the next day, whether you're having a bad day or not, list 10 things you're grateful for. Add these to the previous list, or start a new one. The third time, I challenge you to make a list of 15 things you appreciate. I encourage you to do this for twenty days until you've made a list of at least 100 things that are working in your life. If you do this exercise in earnest, I assure you that you'll shift from stuck to mobile, from negative to positive. You'll remove the shackles of cynicism, and set yourself free to conquer all you truly dream.

16

Create Wealth By Giving More Away

The Giving of Getting

Great leaders give.

They give all the time. They look for places to give. They don't fear being taken advantage of because their experience tells them that giving has inherent good results.

Nor do these leaders look for someone to notice the giving. Even when no one would ever notice, they give anyway. They do it because the habit is self-rewarding and has become ingrained in a great leader's way of being.

Maybe sometimes you get tired because you think you've given all you can give. But you actually have much more to give than you think, because you have more energy than you think. The more you extend yourself in true service, the more energy comes back around. There's a natural compensating flow to the order of giving. Therefore great leadership is never stingy. It's steeped in generosity.

This is why I lead people to always find something they love to do. The more you love what you do each day, the more you'll want to share yourself with the people you work with and the people you serve.

You won't feel the urge to keep track of how much service you render to others, because keeping track detracts from the joy of the service itself.

Unfortunately the world has no shortage of lazy people. Somewhere along the way they begin to keep score on how much they're giving and what they think they should be getting back. Soon they decide they may have been betrayed. So they stop sharing themselves with others, as if they'll find repayment in their own withholding.

But holding back from others backs up on us. It keeps us stuck in a rut of blame and resentment. We think we're protecting what we have by not giving it away. But when we hold onto our gifts, refusing to share them, they begin to rot and shrink within us, costing us energy. We lose more than anyone else ever cost us. When we decide to hold out until we receive what we're owed, we hurt no one but ourselves.

If you want out of that jail of self-deception, I invite you to find someone or something to whom you can give everything in your power. Find a worthy project or person and give until it hurts. I recommend putting so much inspiration and enthusiasm into this project that you reach a point where you don't think you can give any more.

Don't do it to be noticed. Instead, look to see how you experience yourself.

Don't look for instant remuneration, either. Because indulging greed and materialism steals away the giving nature of your actions. They have now changed from giving to trading. Not nearly the same thing.

This doesn't mean you have to give away every dime you have or everything you own, so that you're penniless, homeless, and hungry—there's no point in making yourself into a needy case so that you have nothing left to give. I'm simply talking about giving in ways that can make a real difference in the life of someone else.

When you give all you can to someone else, you will fill up with energy and other gifts that will help you move to the next level in life. The dam of resentment and negativity that stands between you and "getting" becomes unblocked by your "giving."

At any given moment, I know plenty of people who are stuck, giving up on giving until they start getting. How do they get unstuck? They give even though they fear they have nothing left to offer. They give to someone who is more stuck than they are. They listen to them. They assist them. They serve those people and they soon feel the powerful shifts that take place in their own state of being.

Give enough, and you'll be lifted free from whatever has been holding you back.

Your life's purpose will reassert itself and become clear again.

It's like lifting weights. It hurts, but it hurts to good purpose. You may think you've given and given and given, and you're all given out. But let me tell you something: if you think that, you just may be under a little too much influence from the age of entitlement.

Many people born after the Depression era have gone soft on the subject of giving, believing they should only put in so much effort before sitting back and waiting to receive satisfaction and fulfillment as their just deserts. I'm here to tell you that if you really want to receive something meaningful, you can never stop giving.

You can't keep looking over your shoulder waiting for everyone else to catch up and give you what you think you're owed. You're looking in the wrong direction—you'll rarely receive your reward from the person you originally gave to.

Besides, the greatest gifts you'll receive will come from within. If that's not enough to satisfy you, I have some bad news for you: nothing ever will.

It's when we recognize that the abundant gifts in our lives were there the whole time that we begin to have the power of happiness in our hands. Until we can see that, any effort at fulfillment is like throwing water into a colander. It keeps slipping through the holes, leaving us empty.

On the other hand, if you're doing your best to hang in there and give others all you have, but you feel alienated from the people you give to, you'll be glad to know there's a shift at hand in the world.

In an increasingly global society, we often find ourselves surrounded by people with such varied belief systems, interests, and capabilities that we can feel alone, divided from those around us by occupational, spiritual, familial, social, political, and financial differences. But part of getting real is our willingness to accept this fact, and see the gift in it.

Because as we become increasingly at home in this global society, we have increasing opportunity to reflect on this evolution of differences, and to see that there is a great gift possible in the intersection of so many ideas. When we're willing to give from the heart even when we don't know the hearts of others, to mutually share ideas even when they differ, we have an opportunity to gain a new understanding of each other. We begin to bring together the best of our various ideas into a new whole.

What do you as a leader get from putting yourself out there? You get yourself back. You obtain abilities improved by experience. You experience new confidence built by the changes you've effected in the world. You feel a spirit inspired by what others bring to the table when you inspire them. The energy you give away comes back to you, and then some, so you can do it again tomorrow.

True Service

Would you be willing to "fire" a client if you thought firing them would serve them?

What if that action meant leaving thousands of dollars on the table?

For example: imagine that you were a plastic surgeon and a patient came to you asking for liposuction, when they were already perfectly slim and it was obvious they were seeking unnecessary surgery because they suffered from low self-esteem. Would you tell your patient the truth or would you go for the money?

What is your willingness to really serve other people, instead of giving them what they say they want regardless of the consequences? Do you offer people what you know they need, based on the expertise for which they sought you?

Most of us are afraid to serve on that profound a level. We serve others when it is convenient for us, or at best, when they ask us. What about the times when it's not convenient, or when they clearly don't know what their options are and therefore don't know what to ask for?

In the past, I was terrified to truly serve others. To me being of service equated with being subservient, which put the other person in a position of power and control over me. I feared that service might put me in a position of weakness and vulnerability. To me, looking only to be of service was the same as inviting people to take advantage of me. Or, if I was of service in the ways that I believed I should and could be, I feared they might not approve of my outspoken form of leading.

Now I can see how misguided my thinking was. It was based on fear and mistrust.

Today I see the spirit of service more clearly. Service as I see it today begins with my listening to someone with my heart and then letting my instincts guide me, so that I can help them pursue their best path with strength and courage.

There was another belief I had to shift before I could be of real service to others.

I used to think it was safest to keep all negative thoughts to myself, to assume that people couldn't handle uncomfortable truths. But when I looked underneath that, I saw that I wasn't really worried about whether they could handle the truth, but about whether I could.

Once I began to handle the truth in my own life, I found it easier to share the truth more fully with my clients and the people around me. Today I realize that I need to give people more credit, and to return the power of choice to them.

If I see a truth that they don't see and I think it can serve them, as someone who has promised to be of service I owe it to them to share what I see. What they do with the information is up to them.

This doesn't hurt them—it empowers them. It puts them in the driver's seat. Whereas when I withheld important information from people, it was a cowardly way to maintain subtle control over the relationship. Some people call this kind of behavior passive-aggressive. It pretends to be of service, yet it's a way to control a situation without taking responsibility for the results.

When I committed to telling even the most difficult truths in service to others, I created the largest client base I've seen in my 20 years of teaching leadership.

People may get their noses slightly bent out of shape the first time I tell them the truth, but ultimately they're relieved to find that I'm not a yes-man. I'm someone they know they can trust. If I'm willing to tell them the bad news, they can trust when I tell them the good. If I'm willing to tell them the bad news, they also now have options to make changes for the better.

As I get older I'm willing to go to almost any degree to serve other human beings. I get juiced up from it. Service to others serves me.

Service is the bedrock of any thriving business.

Think about it: Would you follow a leader who was unwilling to serve others? If a leader told you something about yourself that no one ever told you before, even something painful, and if the information allowed you to change in ways that enhanced your ability to grow, wouldn't you invite that person back the next time you were seeking growth in your life?

Here's the thing: You know when you're being served and when you're being played. You can feel the difference. When someone is telling you the truth to be of service to you, their motive is clear: They are helping you get real. They are presenting the reality that will help you change the condition they are so honest and direct about. They have nothing to gain themselves except the gift of inspiring you.

If you are a leader, you'll understand that service is not about controlling another person. In fact, when we're in true service we care only about putting the gift out there, and we let go of the results.

Team members who want to be empowered will see the leadership in you. People who are afraid of their own power will disappear and never return. That's OK, because you can't contribute to people who don't want to receive. Just as I can't coach people who are not open to being coached.

Leadership requires trust in ourselves and in those we serve. So once you've found someone willing, offer all you have to give, without reservation. You'll receive exponential returns.

Get Real

As you conclude this final chapter, please grab one more piece of paper, but this time make it a scrap, something just big enough for you to write one sentence on it. Now, I invite you to consider the subject that I hope was at the heart of your desire to read this book. Just for a moment, set aside whatever you think people have always expected of you, set aside everything you've done up to this moment, set aside your desire for approval. Now, think of the word "service." If you had one person you could serve, who would that be? Write that person's name down.

If you could offer that person just one service, a service you could put your heart and soul into, a service you know you're capable of offering, a service that you get excited just thinking about—what would it be? Write down your answer in a single sentence.

What is the first step that would take you in the direction of that service? Don't write that down onto the sheet of paper. Grab your calendar or to-do list, pick a date and write the first step there.

After you finish that first step, decide what is the second step that will lead you in the direction of that service, and schedule it for the earliest possible date you can. After that, move to step three, and so on, until you have completed your service to that person. When you've finished your service, pick another person and start again.

———————————————

Recommended Coaches

*I have worked with or know each of these coaches personally
and I highly recommend them for services rendered.*
~ Stephen McGhee

Get Real blends the emotional and spiritual with intellectual
and then steps through very applicable and sustainable examples to help leaders' breakthrough barriers to a prosperous
life of inspirational leadership. *Get Real* provides a pragmatic
approach to elevating your game TODAY. Stephen nails it
and you will feel it. How to succeed in Life and Leadership?
GET REAL.

~ Greg Aden, Founder, Aden Leadership
www.adenleadership.com

Stephen's gift is helping others to trust their true selves. To
forget what everyone else thinks or says they should do. To
be authentic. To trust yourself more than you trust other
people. Since embracing this way of being, my fulfillment in
life and ability to serve my clients has attained levels I've
never before thought possible.

~ Brad Billingsley, Success and Performance Coach
www.successproject.net

Having been coached by Stephen, I can say that reading *Get
Real* is an experience similar to sitting across from him.

Stephen and his delivery of "the truth talk" is as authentic as it gets. His authenticity opened my eyes to who I am as a soulful leader and motivator.

~ Joe Burtoni, Businessoul Coach/Real Estate Broker

www.durangolandandhomes.com

Stephen McGhee gives it to us straight. *Get Real* is a page-turning book of current day wisdom filled with key points leading us straight toward the light between man and God. He encourages us to move enthusiastically; he suggests we "BE" with a deeper intention, and he shows us that to slow down and see through the noise tells us we are the only ones in our own way.

~ Marty Chapman, Leadership Development Coach

www.thelifecouncil.com

In my view success is not about the summit. It's stumbling and still continuing to climb. *Get Real* is the catalyst for taking that next step—your next step. Read it and step into action.

~ Molly Fiore, Author of *Opting In*

www.pkexcellence.com

I love this Reality! Stephen McGhee writes as he coaches: with laser-like clarity. Every chapter of this book is a foundation for a Life of Excellence. The piece on Create Something from Nothing is worth the price of admission alone.

~ David Firth, Author of *Change Your*

Organization One Word at a Time

www.davidfirth.com

Wherever you are in life, whatever you do and in whatever capacity, know that you are in a leadership position. Here, within the valuable pages of Stephen McGhee's *Get Real* book, are powerful, practical and proven ways for you to reach the top of your leadership capabilities.

~ Raja Hireker, Big Idea Creator &
Communications Specialist,
www.RajaHireker.com

Finally, here is a leadership book that cuts through all the rhetoric and hype of false and misleading inspiration. As any great and powerful visionary knows—the final test of excellence of any leader is the ability to produce sustainable and impactful results the serves the highest good of all. Stephen McGhee takes you straight into the heart and soul of the path to Leadership Excellence.

~ Tom LaRotonda, Life Coach, Author of
Only Love Is Real
www.tomlarotonda.com

For most of my life I have been a disciple of Leadership and Performance. While much of what I have read has been valuable, this book has a rare combination of experience and application. If you apply the principles in this book, you will not be able to avoid powerful and positive change. There are principles in this book that have assisted me into unparalleled levels of personal and professional success. Not

simply tools, but applications that have you being the leader of your own life. Hold on tight...
> ~ Jeff Patterson, Success and Leadership Coach,
> Aspen Success Coaching
> www.Aspensuccesscoaching.com

I have been a devoted student of leadership and performance for over twenty years. While I've read many good books and worked with top performance coaches, Stephen brings a truly unique and holistic approach to achieving success in life and in business. He is a pioneer for the new paradigm of leadership. I encourage anyone to read this book who wants to take their life to the next level, to truly step into a reality of abundance, joy, freedom, peace of mind, and happiness, and get real.
> ~ Keith Walters, Holistic Lifestyle Coach, Entrepreneur,
> Former Professional Athlete

A well respected writer, centuries ago, penned something along the lines of "My people perish for lack of vision." While possibly taken out of context, I've used this as a marker in my life to ensure I was creating my future as opposed to letting life happen to me. In this chapter, Stephen talks about creating the Big Commitment, aligning your actions towards achieving it and eliminating the distractions. My experience is that highly successful people in all walks of life follow this sage advice.

> ~ John Wittry
> http://relationshiprestoration.wordpress.com/

About The Author

Stephen McGhee is the CEO of Stephen McGhee Leadership, Inc. He is a Visionary Leadership Guide to fortune 500 managers across the globe. His business is devoted to supporting those individuals in becoming highly influential leaders whom then leave a positive and sustainable legacy. Stephen has consulted with progressive corporations and their top-level personnel for more than 20 years, sharing his expertise through outcome-focused initiatives, such as planning sessions, culture-change engagements and his one to one "Velocity Sessions".

With 10 years as a senior executive in the financial services arena, Stephen assists leaders in converting their individual potential and enhanced collaboration of their teams. He offers a degree in finance, and a master's degree in spiritual psychology. This combination brings a grounded blend between the reality of today and the possibility of tomorrow.

Stephen is an author of several books and a documentary film, called *Climb for Freedom: Seven Men's Journey from the Ordinary to the Extraordinary*, which chronicles a comprehensive year-long leadership program that culminated in the summit of the highest mountain in the world outside of Asia. You may learn more at www.mcgheeleadership.com or by email at stephen@mcgheeleadership.com

45151760R00119

Made in the USA
San Bernardino, CA
01 February 2017